HIKING WASHINGTON'S
FIRE
LOOKOUTS

HIKING WASHINGTON'S
FIRE
LOOKOUTS

AMBER CASALI

MOUNTAINEERS
BOOKS

MOUNTAINEERS BOOKS is the publishing division of The Mountaineers, an organization founded in 1906 and dedicated to the exploration, preservation, and enjoyment of outdoor and wilderness areas.

1001 SW Klickitat Way, Suite 201, Seattle, WA 98134
800-553-4453, www.mountaineersbooks.org

Printed in China
Distributed in the United Kingdom by Cordee, www.cordee.co.uk

First edition, 2018

Copyeditor: Ginger Everhart
Design and layout: Jen Grable
Cartographer: Martha Bostwick

All photographs by the author unless otherwise noted
Cover photographs, clockwise from upper left: *Western anemone on trail to Winchester Mountain Lookout; Granite Mountain Lookout; Firefinder at Mount Leecher Lookout; Winchester Mountain Lookout*
Frontispiece: *On the trail up to Granite Mountain Lookout*

The background maps for this book were produced using the online map viewer CalTopo. For more information, visit caltopo.com.

Library of Congress Cataloging-in-Publication Data
Names: Casali, Amber, author.
Title: Hiking Washington's fire lookouts / Amber Casali.
Description: First edition. | Seattle, WA : Mountaineers Books, [2018] |
    Includes bibliographical references and index.
Identifiers: LCCN 2017036731| ISBN 9781680510607 (pbk) |
    ISBN 9781680510614 (ebook)
Subjects: LCSH: Hiking—Washington (State)—Guidebooks. | Fire
    lookouts—Washington (State)—Guidebooks. | Washington (State)—Guidebooks.
Classification: LCC GV199.42.W2 C37 2018 | DDC 796.5109797—dc23
LC record available at https://lccn.loc.gov/2017036731

Printed on FSC®-certified materials

MIX
Paper from
responsible sources
FSC® C008047

Mountaineers Books titles may be purchased for corporate, educational, or other promotional sales, and our authors are available for a wide range of events. For information on special discounts or booking an author, contact our customer service at 800-553-4453 or mbooks@mountaineersbooks.org.

ISBN (paperback): 978-1-68051-060-7
ISBN (ebook): 978-1-68051-061-4

CONTENTS

NORTH

CENTRAL

SOUTH

OLYMPICS

LOOKOUTS AT A GLANCE

LOOKOUT	ROUNDTRIP DISTANCE	ELEVATION GAIN	LOOKOUT ELEVATION
NORTH			
1. Mount Constitution	6.6 miles	1490 feet	2407 feet
2. Winchester Mountain	3.4 miles	1300 feet	6510 feet
3. Copper Ridge	19.4 miles	5300 feet	6260 feet
4. Park Butte	7.5 miles	2190 feet	5459 feet
5. Lookout Mountain (Cascade River Road)	9.4 miles	4480 feet	5719 feet
6. Hidden Lake	8 miles	3280 feet	6890 feet
7. Sourdough Mountain	10.6 miles	5090 feet	5985 feet
8. Desolation Peak	45.2 miles	4400 feet	6102 feet
9. North Mountain	2.4 miles	570 feet	3824 feet
10. Green Mountain	8.4 miles	3300 feet	6500 feet
11. Miners Ridge	30.6 miles	4610 feet	6208 feet
12. Mount Pilchuck	5.4 miles	2200 feet	5324 feet
13. Three Fingers	15 miles	4200 feet	6850 feet
14. Monument 83	19 miles	2840 feet	6520 feet
15. Slate Peak	0.7 mile	280 feet	7440 feet
16. Goat Peak	3.5 miles	1400 feet	7001 feet
17. North Twentymile	12.6 miles	4390 feet	7437 feet
18. Lookout Mountain (Methow Valley)	3.2 miles	1150 feet	5515 feet
19. Mount Leecher	2.5 miles	520 feet	5008 feet
20. Buck Mountain	4 miles	1160 feet	6135 feet
21. Funk Mountain	0.4 mile	160 feet	5121 feet
22. Mount Bonaparte	5.2 miles	2210 feet	7257 feet

LOOKOUT	ROUNDTRIP DISTANCE	ELEVATION GAIN	LOOKOUT ELEVATION
CENTRAL			
23. Heybrook Mountain	2.2 miles	890 feet	1739 feet
24. Evergreen Mountain	2.6 miles	1370 feet	5587 feet
25. Alpine Lookout	9.8 miles	3000 feet	6235 feet
26. Sugarloaf Peak	1 mile	180 feet	5814 feet
27. Tyee Mountain	6.6 miles	1530 feet	6654 feet
28. Granite Mountain	8 miles	3800 feet	5629 feet
29. Thorp Mountain	7 miles	2290 feet	5854 feet
30. Red Top Mountain	1 mile	330 feet	5361 feet
SOUTH			
31. Kelly Butte	3.2 miles	1050 feet	5413 feet
32. Sun Top	1 mile	450 feet	5271 feet
33. Tolmie Peak	5.6 miles	1000 feet	5925 feet
34. Mount Fremont	5.6 miles	800 feet	7181 feet
35. Gobblers Knob	7 miles	1000 feet	5485 feet
36. Shriner Peak	8.4 miles	3420 feet	5834 feet
37. High Rock	3 miles	1330 feet	5685 feet
38. Burley Mountain	15 miles	4020 feet	5304 feet
39. Jump Off Mountain	7.4 miles	1550 feet	5670 feet
40. Red Mountain	6.8 miles	1620 feet	4965 feet
OLYMPICS			
41. Kloshe Nanitch and North Point	0.8 mile	190 feet	3160 and 3340 feet
42. Pyramid Mountain	7.4 miles	2400 feet	3100 feet
43. Dodger Point	28 miles	4890 feet	5760 feet
44. Ned Hill	2 miles	910 feet	3458 feet

INTRODUCTION

Lookouts have much to offer. For hikers, they guarantee views from the top. For historians, they share a glimpse into Washington's past. For naturalists and biologists, they teach lessons about forest-fire management. For poets, they represent the wildest parts of our state juxtaposed with the manmade idea of home.

My first fire-lookout visit in Washington was Park Butte. We went on an overnight, and pitched our tents in the camping area a half mile below. At the lookout, we chatted with other hikers and gazed at the stunning view. Then suddenly, everyone was gone. It was a Saturday night in August, and to my amazement, no one was sleeping in the open lookout. It was everything I could do to tear myself away from that deck as the sun glistened and sank lower toward the river valley. Just as a friend back in Bellingham had told me, it was an incredible spot, exactly halfway up a mountain—views down the Nooksack River valley to Puget Sound and the Olympics and views to the glaciers on Mount Baker's south side and the North Cascades beyond. All in one place.

Of course, that first trip was a dream scenario—but I was hooked. Many lookouts may already be full when you get there, and some cannot be safely entered at all. For better or worse, that's part of what makes lookouts so intriguing: their condition and remoteness run the gamut. It's also what makes them such good hiking destinations. You can hike to a lookout that is a mile up a wide, gravel road or twenty miles down a narrow trail—and everything in between. You can rent some lookouts online; others you can sleep in by simply showing up. There are those you can visit only for the day—camping prohibited—and those you are barred from visiting at all. Some are maintained and in pristine condition; others have been forgotten for decades and are sagging into disrepair.

One thing I know for sure: you should visit them while you can. At the height of Washington's forest-fire-spotting program, there were between 500 and 600 backcountry lookout structures in the state. Now we have 89, having lost several just in the past few years. I can't tell you how many times during my research I came across pictures or stories or books about amazing lookouts only to find that they

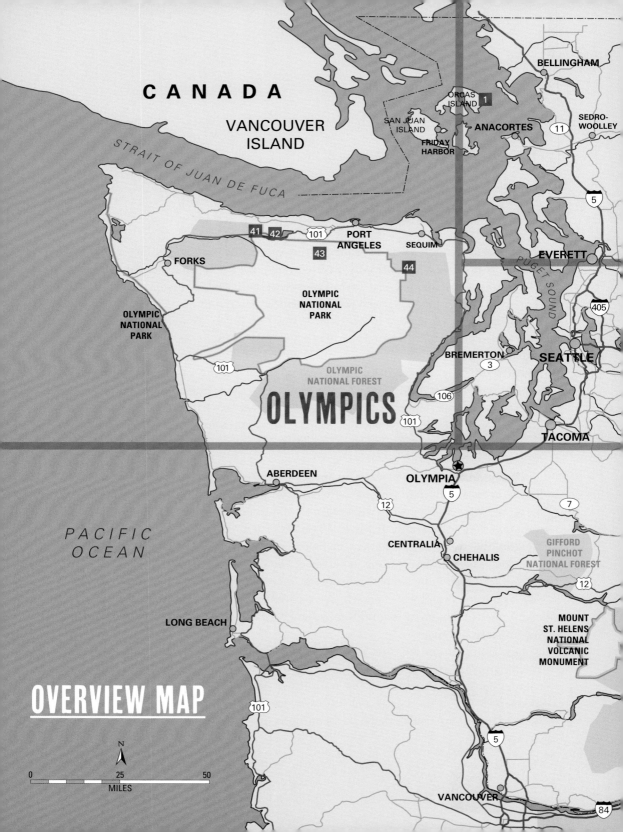

OVERVIEW MAP

MILES
0   25   50

Trail to Winchester Mountain Lookout

are no longer standing. As ecstatic as I have been to explore the wealth of remaining lookouts, I have a profound sense of loss when I read about all the lookouts that have already disappeared. Enjoy the gems that are still standing, whether you drive, day hike, or backpack to get there. And consider donating to the organizations supporting lookouts or even getting involved in lookout maintenance through volunteer work parties (mentioned in lookout descriptions where applicable).

A BRIEF HISTORY OF WASHINGTON'S FIRE LOOKOUTS

The West was unfamiliar territory when settlers first came out. Pioneers did not arrive with generations of knowledge on what was typical for forest fires. It took a few really big burns in the late 1800s and early 1900s and the loss of personal and commercial property (mostly valuable timberlands) before the federal government formed the US Forest Service in 1905. The agency's work made forest conservation a national priority, developing the foundations for preventing, spotting, and fighting fires on public forest lands.

Many fires were caused by sparks from trains that ran through forested areas, an unforeseen consequence of railroad expansion. Mining activities and campfires often resulted in fires as well. Of course, lightning strikes are a common cause, too, especially in the eastern foothills of the Cascades. The cool, wet air from the Pacific Ocean moves over the mountains and meets the warm, dry air of the Eastern Washington plateau, which creates lightning. Whatever the cause of the fire, early detection was crucial to minimizing loss of livelihoods and lives.

This approach to spotting and stopping fires was done with the best of intentions. However, we learned through the century that fire is an essential part of the local ecology. Ponderosa pines are very fire resistant, with thick bark and without lower branches, so fire has a hard time climbing up the trees. Fire thins the forest understory, creating sunny spots for flowers and wildlife to thrive. Burned trees house insects, providing food for birds. Many plants have adapted to their fire-prone areas and need fire for dormant seeds to germinate or to stimulate flowering. Fire also promotes decomposition and nutrient recycling in dry climates. And, when humans suppress the regular small-burn cycles, excess fuel accumulates in forests, making the burns that do happen even more catastrophic. There is no easy solution; modern forest managers seek to understand the cycles of a healthy forest ecosystem while also protecting people and resources.

LEFT *Remnants of the ladder leading to original Mount Leecher crow's nest* **RIGHT** *Original structure at North Twentymile, the only remaining cupola in the Washington Cascades, with view obscured by wildfire smoke*

TYPES OF LOOKOUTS AND CONSTRUCTION TIMELINE

Fire watching from mountaintops in the Pacific Northwest began around 1914. At that time, most lookout sites were "rag camps," where the staff lived in a tent, cooked outside, and watched for fires from a high spot in a nearby tree, often from a wooden platform called a "crow's nest." You can still see two intact crow's nests in the Methow Valley, at Mount Leecher and Funk Mountain, both nearly a century old.

Next came cabins with cupolas—small domes or turrets on top of a roof. Pro tip: Pay attention to the roof shape to get a good idea of the lookout type and how old it is. Cupolas in Washington were often a D-6 design, named after US Forest Service District 6 in California. These were among the earliest constructed lookouts, starting in the 1920s, where staff lived in the cabins and watched for fires from the slightly elevated vantage points above the roofs. Many of the lookout sites in this book had cupolas: Sourdough Mountain, Kelly Butte, Lookout Mountain (Cascade River Road), Jump Off Mountain, North Point, and Red Top Mountain to name a few. They are historic and elegant and, unfortunately, very few still exist. You can see a wooden cabin with a sheet-metal cupola at Monument 83, a stone's throw from the newer tower lookout, but it's on the Canadian side of the US-Canada border. The only remaining cupola in the Washington Cascades is North Twentymile in the Methow Valley—also alongside a newer tower on the site.

The classic design that you will see most commonly today are the L-4 cabs, built in the 1930s at the height of lookout construction. The L-4 is typically fourteen feet by fourteen feet with windows on all four sides, hinged shutters that lift up and are propped in place, and one door. The L-4s represent the golden era of lookout construction, when massive funding and labor were available thanks to the New Deal's Civilian Conservation Corps (CCC). A few days after Franklin Delano Roosevelt became president of the United States in 1933, he proposed a solution to the country's high unemployment rate, telling Congress:

> I propose to create a civilian conservation corps to be used in simple work, not interfering with normal employment, and confining itself to forestry, the prevention of soil erosion, flood control and other similar projects. . . . More important than the material gains will be the moral and spiritual value of such work. The overwhelming majority of unemployed Americans, who are now walking the streets and receiving private or public relief, would infinitely prefer to work.

Within five months of being established, the CCC had more than a quarter million young men enrolled to work for the initial six-month period, assigned to one of 1400 work camps around the country. The CCC came to an end in 1942, when Congress denied future funding for any more projects. But by that time, there were more than 600 lookouts in Washington State, and 8000 lookouts nationwide.

World War II added a new aspect to lookout history. Several lookouts that had been built in the previous decade were used for spotting warplanes (instead of fires) for the US Army's Aircraft Warning Service (AWS). There were around 100 AWS watch sites on the US Pacific coast in the early 1940s. Since the AWS postings were year-round, it meant that these structures, intended for summertime dwelling, now had wintertime residents—a pretty rugged and challenging undertaking in a shack that was usually around a mile high in elevation.

One memorable story is of a couple who lived for twelve months at Red Mountain in the Gifford Pinchot National Forest in southern Washington starting in the fall of 1942. They had a garage full of wood with a small sleeping room attached. They took turns sleeping while one person kept watch from the fire lookout. It started snowing in late October, and the lookout location was under snow until mid-July. Fog kept them socked in, ice snapped the phone lines, and the privy was regularly buried

Sunset view of Mount Baker from trail to Hidden Lake Lookout

under snow. High winds frequently would blow out the oil stove and cause the chimney to fill with snow. Despite the amount of work the basic daily tasks entailed, the orders from their superiors were to melt more snow for water and chop more wood. Wood chopped from that season was still there forty years later!

Although, before the war, it was not unheard of for women to work as solo staff and perform all the same duties as men, the war years saw more women applying to staff fire lookouts. Often they were schoolteachers who had summers off. The number of female staff increased significantly during World War II, as more women were hired to do work traditionally considered to be in the men's sphere. It was also common for married couples (including some adventurous honeymooners) to staff lookouts together.

Lookouts from the 1920s and '30s were primarily "ground houses," built directly on the summit, often using local rock to help form a flatter foundation. Towers were built in the '40s, '50s, and '60s, often with L-4 cabs on top and the addition of "catwalks" or wraparound decks. On almost all tower structures, there are stairs for entering the catwalks from below through a trapdoor, and the catwalks lead to the cabins' entrances. Very few ground houses have catwalks, except Mount Pilchuck (where its rocky perch makes it unsafe to walk around the base of the building), Tyee Mountain, Kelly Butte, and Thorp Mountain near Cle Elum (which has a catwalk on two and a half sides).

A later design, the R-6 (named after US Forest Service Region 6), was first constructed in 1953. R-6 lookouts are typically fifteen feet by fifteen feet and have flat roofs that overhang the cabin to provide shade. Most R-6 cabs were placed atop towers but can also function as ground houses.

Most of the structures seen today are the second, third, or fourth structure on the site. There were very few lookouts built after the mid-twentieth century, and in fact, many lookouts were closed during that period as fire-watch culture and technology changed. During the 1960s and '70s, the US Forest Service stopped maintaining many of the defunct lookout buildings, and the structures became a liability.

The vantage points that make the views so amazing come at a price for the buildings. The structures are subjected to high winds, extreme weather, and constant deterioration. They need regular maintenance, often more labor hours than budgeted for by the Forest Service or the National Park Service. When lookouts were staffed, even for just a few months of the year, there was a person on-site full-time who could replace window panes, touch up paint, and do any carpentry repairs. But once the buildings were no longer used annually, their fates began to vary wildly.

For many no-longer-active lookouts, there simply is not funding or staffing to maintain them to safety standards. Ironically, after dutifully serving lifetimes in the prevention of fires, these structures end up being intentionally burned to the ground. Beginning in the 1970s, organizations began adopting lookouts to help maintain them. In some cases existing organizations, such as a local Alpine Club or Mountaineers chapter, adopted a nearby lookout; other times a "Friends of" group formed by local citizens worked to preserve a lookout. These dedicated groups often restored lookouts sufficiently enough for them to be added to the National Register of Historic Places, in addition to providing ongoing care and attention. A few lookouts are still staffed, and some in the national parks are maintained and used as needed by the Park Service. Most of the rest have been forgotten, and there is no telling what their destinies might be.

THE AGELESS TOOL FOR PINPOINTING FIRE LOCATIONS

The US Forest Service has been using one piece of equipment for pinpointing the locations of fires for more than a century, and it is still used today with incredible accuracy: the Osborne Firefinder. It was invented in 1915 by W. B. Osborne, a Forest

LEFT *Crosshairs on the firefinder at Alpine Lookout* **RIGHT** *Larger map for pinpointing fire location beyond the firefinder radius*

Service employee based in Portland, Oregon. The firefinder is a type of alidade, used to sight a distant object and measure its angle in relation to something else. Basically, the firefinder consists of a map oriented to true north that extends for a 20-mile radius from the fire lookout, which is mapped dead center. Each map square is one mile. The firefinder is round and is encircled by two rings—an inner one that moves and an outer one with fixed markers. There are two vertical sights that rise from opposite points on the outer edge of the firefinder; one is an elevation marker, and the other, the crosshairs.

A firefinder is placed on a stand, which is mounted on tracks and pivots in the middle of the lookout building, allowing the whole firefinder to be adjusted and remain level. The lookout staff sights the fire in the crosshairs of the finder and moves the vertical and horizontal parts to get a heading in degrees, or the azimuth. Then staff pinpoints the fire's distance from the lookout on the map, based on topography and the inch scale markers.

To get the most accurate reading, it's important that the crosshairs are in good condition for the lookout staff to accurately sight the smoke. One staffer told me that string would be too thick, and metal would rust too easily. "It's government-issued horsehair," he said, before adding with a smile, "That's probably a term you didn't know you would hear today." For places where the visibility is greater than 20 miles, staff need a map that covers a larger area than the one on the firefinder. They use a large flat map instead, but with the same orientation of the lookout in the middle of the map and a means to measure degrees to pinpoint a smoke site. The map may be hung on the ceiling or pulled out as needed and placed on the bed.

"SISTER" LOOKOUTS

A firefinder is useful on its own, but staff could get even more precise measurements by coordinating with what I call "sister" lookouts. These are lookouts set within sight of each other for maximum surveillance and fire location accuracy. Few sister groups survive, but often one sister of a group is still standing Each lookout description indicates if other lookouts are visible from the summit.

Even the most remote lookout in the state, Desolation Peak, could see the lamplights from Crater Mountain Lookout (no longer standing) and Sourdough Mountain. Continuing east on State Route 20, there were at least thirty-five lookouts in the Methow Valley *alone*. Now there are just a handful. And even if you can see a structure, so few lookouts are still staffed that they are no longer being used as true sister lookouts. There is only one person employed to staff the three sister lookouts at Lookout Mountain (Methow Valley), Mount Leecher, and Goat Peak. There is no way to coordinate firefinder measurements if two out of the three lookouts are unoccupied. But one place where triangulation could still happen is off US Highway 2 near Leavenworth. Alpine Lookout on Nason Ridge is still staffed, as is Sugarloaf Peak. They are within sight of each other, and even if the staff have never met in person, they talk on the radio and would be able to work together to give joint azimuth readings if necessary.

THE EVOLUTION OF FIRE-REPORTING COMMUNICATION AND TECHNOLOGY

Before telephones or radios, staff reported fires to receiving stations up to thirty miles away using the sun's rays reflected onto a mirrored device called a heliograph. Staff used the movable mirror and shutters of the device to flash Morse code between lookout towers.

Then came phone lines and hand-cranked telephones, which required running a physical line of heavy-gauge steel wire from the summit to the nearest guard station. Staff had to maintain miles of lines that required a lot of upkeep and, unfortunately, were excellent conductors. To avoid being on the receiving end of a lightning strike, staff used a "kill" switch or quick disconnect to detach the wire from the lookout phone during an electrical storm. You can still see many places along forest trails where the original ceramic insulators were hung to run the phone lines from lookouts to guard stations. When visiting lookouts, keep an eye out for white or brown round objects in trees about eight feet off the ground.

World War II brought two major technological changes. First, radio technology was more developed, making lines for phones obsolete. After the war there was surplus radio equipment, and though cumbersome, radio systems became more portable.

Second, observation planes became more commonplace, and as fuel was inexpensive, aerial surveillance slowly began to replace humans on mountaintops. In some cases, it became cheaper to fly airplanes than to train people and staff lookouts all season. By the 1950s and '60s, fewer and fewer lookouts were staffed each summer.

People in planes, however, are not as effective at spotting fires as trained observers on the ground. Lookout staff learn the surrounding topography intimately and can immediately spot the smallest change in the landscape. Planes move very quickly and are flown by pilots who do not have the extensive observational experience of living in the particular place they observe from the air. Considering the cost associated with flight these days, staffing lookouts with humans is still the most efficient, cost-effective way to spot forest fires.

Another development was radio repeater technology. The radio equipment that lookout staff use operates at a frequency above the FM band, because the shorter radio wavelengths are not very effective at reaching through mountains and canyons, and function best in line-of-sight configurations. For places that don't have full line of sight, the US Forest Service placed repeater stations at strategic locations to receive, boost, and relay signals from portable radios in the field. Field crews change channels, using trial and error to find the closest line-of-sight repeater that can be heard by them and the dispatch center. When the repeaters don't work well enough, then lookout staff often become "human repeaters" due to their elevation and clear line of sight from the transmitter.

As the technology evolved throughout the twentieth century, radios got smaller. One current-day lookout staffer reports that his handheld radio is about eight inches by one and a half inches by three inches. Most staffed lookouts are equipped with a solar panel hooked up to a 12-volt deep-cycle storage battery, much like a car battery. The battery is solar powered and provides a storage reserve for night and long periods of cloud cover. The storage battery is connected to either an inverter (to make 120-volt AC power) or to a charger base to provide 12-volt power for recharging power packs that fit the radio equipment. With this stored power, staff can also charge small appliances such as cell phones or LED reading lamps.

On large fires that burn for weeks or months, radio techs will often set up portable repeaters on ridgetops or peaks in line of sight with deployed firefighters. Crews can input

Lightning stool with glass feet insulators at Hidden Lake Lookout

fire-specific frequencies on the radio equipment, so that the constant traffic to manage a fire does not tie up the general channels that lookout staff use for daily, routine communications. There are districts in Eastern Washington that use satellite phones when crews or fire camps are in places without good radio repeater or cell tower access.

Starting around 2011, 4G-data coverage became available in more areas where some lookouts are still staffed. No longer so isolated from the rest of the world, staff can read news, exchange email, and post their sunset photos on social media with their smartphones. Though daily radio communication is still the standard, staff can use their phones to talk to other lookout staff or dispatch stations without tying up the radio.

SAFETY: STRUCTURE GROUNDING AND LIGHTNING PROTECTION

If you're in a fire lookout on top of a treeless mountain during a lightning storm, you're probably the tallest thing around, which is right where you want to be. Just kidding—that's pretty much the worst place to be. Because lookout staff are subjecting themselves to a decent likelihood of being in a lightning storm, it's extremely important that the lookout structures are as protected from lightning as possible. The buildings have small lightning rods on their roofs that run down to cables that are buried in the ground, to conduct electricity away from the buildings.

All lookouts were once equipped with a "lightning stool," a tiny wooden stool with glass feet. Since glass does not conduct electricity, it was the safest place for staff to be during a storm. They were instructed to stay on the stool until the lightning passed, which could be frightening and uncomfortable and last for three to four hours at a time. Apparently, if the building does get struck by lightning, there will be a loud cracking noise and it will smell like sulfur. Active lookouts still use these stools.

Slate Peak Lookout in fog

WHAT DOES IT TAKE TO STAFF A LOOKOUT?

You may be wondering if lookout staff are all grizzled mountain hermits. I think it's safe to say that they represent some of Washington's hardiest folks. They live alone at high elevations in extreme weather with the looming threat of fire and an imperative for constant vigilance. Although we may have images of the lookout poet sitting all summer in the windowed cabin penning verses, lookout staff actually have quite a few duties. Here is what they are responsible for:

MEETING BASIC NEEDS. To get water early in the season, staff often melt snow; they drank "cold snow-water" as poet and 1950s lookout Gary Snyder wrote in "Mid-August at Sourdough Mountain Lookout." Later in the season, staff usually have to haul water from a creek, lake, or spring. Before gas heaters and stoves, they had to gather and chop wood for cooking and heating.

PROPERTY MAINTENANCE. Staff attend to any carpentry or other building needs, such as painting. They also take care of the grounds and other structures on the summit and keep the trail clear.

CHECKING IN. They used to call in on the hand-crank phone, but now use the radio to check in with the local guard station at the beginning and end of every day they are on shift, as well as listening in all day for any relevant messages being shared. Over the years radio use extended beyond work into social time. Some places had a daily one-hour window when the radios were "open" and the staff were allowed to talk to each other and have "bull" or "rap" sessions. In the Gifford Pinchot National Forest in the 1960s, a local ranger's wife would read newspaper articles to the surrounding lookout staff to keep them informed about the outside world.

LIGHTNING-STORM SAFETY. Staff monitor coming lightning by counting the seconds from flash to thunderclap. When they estimate that a storm is within five miles, they close the door and windows and remain either on the lightning stool or a bed with plastic or glass footings to provide a nonconductive barrier between them and the floor. Another trick to monitor a coming storm? Staff can tune an AM radio between stations, and lightning will cause a crackle and pop from at least twenty miles away.

POST-STORM VIGILANCE. If there is a lightning storm, staff have to remain extra watchful and keep an eye out for "sleepers," which are fires resulting from lightning strikes that can smolder unnoticed for anywhere from a couple of days to a couple of weeks before becoming a visible blaze.

FIRE SCANNING. Staff are expected to perform a thorough fire check of all surrounding areas every two hours, which can take twenty to thirty minutes. And they are supposed to do a cursory scan every fifteen minutes. "Really, you're doing a constant visual scan all day," one current day staffer told me.

FIRE REPORTING. If they do spot a fire, the staff first use the firefinder to determine the coordinates. Then they call it in to the guard station, as well as record it in a logbook. These days, staff on the eastern slope of the Cascades estimate that they spot and report around ten fires in a season.

NONFIRE REPORTING. Staff, knowing the land so well, are often responsible for reporting things that are not fires but could be mistaken for fire smoke by an average person. For example, some lookouts are near quarries that send plumes of dust into the air. There are clouds called "water dogs" that genuinely look like smoke. Lookout staff can give a heads-up to the guard station about potential false alarms.

WAITING. Beat writer Jack Kerouac staffed the lookout at Desolation Peak in the summer of 1956. In his account of the experience in his book *The Dharma Bums*, Kerouac's main character comments on a very real and common impediment to firewatching: "Well, how can I see any fires? There's nothing but fog out there."

Even with all the bustle of daily life, many staff still have time, especially in the evenings, to read, write, reflect, and observe.

....

A couple of things current lookout staff are no longer responsible for:

FIREFIGHTING. Some fire-lookout staff also had firefighting duties, and were called lookout firemen. After calling in a fire, they headed into the forest to dig a fire line to prevent the fire's spread.

PHONE-LINE UPKEEP. The lines were susceptible to being knocked out by lightning or storms, and staff had to regularly walk the length of the phone lines to detect any possible issues. In their book *Lookouts*, Ira Spring and Byron Fish relate the process one former lookout staffer told them:

> It was not always easy to locate the break in insulated wire, but [the Desolation lookout staffer] described one method used if anybody came along to help him. You had him crank the telephone every five seconds while he went down along the line, pinching into the wire. You knew the

Former privy door at Desolation Peak

break was somewhere between you and the lookout when you stopped getting a shock.

Considering that lookouts are located all across the state, it's important to remember that the experiences of lookout staff has varied considerably both by geography and era. Some staff saw almost no humans all summer; others had regular visitors. One young man working on Mount Pugh off the Mountain Loop Highway would run up to ten miles into Darrington every Saturday night to take his girlfriend dancing. Then he would run back up the mountain so that he could radio in and be back on duty by daybreak on Sunday mornings. Even during his very solitary summer on Desolation Peak in the 1950s, Jack Kerouac once hung out with staff down at the Ross Lake Resort when he needed a break and some social interaction.

At the start of the season, in some places, all the supplies are brought in for the summer, and that's it. Other locations get regular resupplies. Even how supplies are delivered varies considerably, by all-terrain vehicle (ATV), helicopter, truck, or even—still—by pack mules, which were used in supplying Alpine Lookout in 2016.

Finally, today, the work of fire-lookout staff varies year to year, depending on what the fire season is like. The Washington Cascades experienced devastating fire seasons in 2014 and '15—millions of acres burned, citizens and firefighters lost their lives, and lookout staff had to be evacuated. You can see remnants of these fires from almost all the lookouts in the Methow Valley. Then, 2016 turned out to be unusually mild, and staff were sent home several weeks earlier than usual. We can't predict what nature will do, but we can get out on the trails to enjoy the remaining lookouts.

GENERAL HIKING CONSIDERATIONS

Before you embark, here are a few handy tips and reminders that I've garnered from my time on the trail, both general guidelines as well as lookout specific.

TEN ESSENTIALS

What's a hiking guidebook without talking about the Ten Essentials? Developed by The Mountaineers, the Ten Essentials are always, well, essential on any hike.

1. Navigation
2. Headlamp
3. Sun protection
4. First-aid supplies
5. Knife
6. Fire
7. Shelter
8. Extra clothes
9. Extra food
10. Extra water

While these are all important, a few stand out in particular when talking about lookout hiking. Sun protection will almost always be critical. Lookout hikes usually start in a shaded forest, and then break out onto treeless, open mountaintops. And a fair number of the hikes in this book are on the east side of the Cascades. Always carry ample sun protection.

I can't emphasize extra clothes enough for lookouts. You may be so hot in your T-shirt when you start hiking that you can't even comprehend being cold. *One long-sleeved shirt layer will be enough, surely!* (I've been there.) It's almost unfathomable just how cold a summit can be when it's windy, exposed, and 4000 vertical feet higher than where you started. There is nothing worse than working hard to get to the gorgeous summit only to want to come down immediately because you're freezing in your flimsy layer. Carry extra clothes in your pack, and put on an extra layer or two as soon as you reach the summit; it's easy to become deeply chilled after a few minutes of sitting still, especially if you sweated a lot on the way up. Some hikers even opt to change shirts at a summit to avoid losing body heat to damp fabrics, synthetic or not.

Foraged berries on Miners Ridge, with view of Glacier Peak

Lastly, a word on water. "Extra water" doesn't just mean carrying extra water, but also having a way to treat water in case you need to refill on the trail. Anywhere a water source is mentioned in a hike description, it is always with the assumption that you are properly treating the water first by filtering, boiling, adding iodine, or using another method that effectively kills bacteria such as giardia. I wish life were like the movies, where we could drink straight from a crystal-clear mountain stream, but even the most pristine-looking waters at high elevations are not guaranteed to be bacteria-free. I also recommend keeping at least a gallon of extra water in your car, for topping off your bottles before you hit the trail and to have waiting when you come back. This is especially important on the east side of the Cascades, where some hikes do not have any water sources.

SEVEN STEPS TO LEAVE NO TRACE

The other guidelines to keep in mind are the Leave No Trace principles and how they relate to lookouts.

PLAN AHEAD AND PREPARE. Know the regulations and special concerns for the area you will visit. Schedule your trip to avoid times of high use—this definitely applies to the more popular, close-to-Seattle hikes in this book. Visit in small groups when possible.

TRAVEL AND CAMP ON DURABLE SURFACES. Durable surfaces include established trails and campsites, rock, gravel, dry grasses, or snow. Take special care in subalpine areas

(4500–8000 feet, which includes pretty much all of the lookouts in this book). The vegetation is extremely fragile and takes a long time to grow back if disturbed.

DISPOSE OF WASTE PROPERLY. This is where "Pack it in, pack it out" fits in. Gone are the days of saying, "But it's biodegradable!" as you toss your apple core or toilet paper into the forest—*everything* should leave with you. In some cases (prepare yourself!), that even means human waste. Some lookout-summit areas do not have a privy and are too small and rocky to dig a proper cat hole. Others have a privy, but they are so overused and undermaintained that the responsible thing to do is pack out waste. Kits for human waste disposal needs while hiking are widely available.

LEAVE WHAT YOU FIND. Enjoy looking at and touching rocks, plants, and other natural objects, but leave things as you found them. The one exception is berries—eat as many as you want while hiking (once you have safely identified them as edible, of course).

MINIMIZE CAMPFIRE IMPACTS. Use a lightweight stove for cooking, and where fires are permitted, use established fire rings, fire pans, or mound fires. For lookout visiting, this issue is especially relevant, as fires are nothing to be casual about. Make sure that all wood is burned to ash, and that you put out the campfires completely.

RESPECT WILDLIFE. Observe wildlife from a distance, but do not approach. Protect wildlife by storing your food, trash, and any other scented items securely. Always check to see if bear canisters are required, and if not, be sure to bring a suitable rope and stuff sack to hang your food out of reach of bears (and other critters) if you are camping. Control pets at all times, or leave them at home. *Note that dogs are prohibited on trails in all national parks.*

BE CONSIDERATE OF OTHERS. Respect other visitors and be courteous. Know the rules of the trail: hikers moving uphill have the right-of-way, step to the downhill side of the trail when encountering pack stock (the animals will stay calmer if you are below rather than above them), and take breaks and make camp away from trails and other visitors.

HOW TO VISIT LOOKOUTS

There are basically five ways that you can visit the lookouts covered in this book, with the vast majority falling under the category of day hiking.

DRIVING. Some lookouts are directly reachable by road and are likely to have open access gates. Any lookouts accessible by car also include a trail approach.

DAY HIKING. All the lookouts offer great vantage points, but levels of access to the building vary. Some lookouts are locked but allow access to the catwalks, which is great, because you can often still see inside and enjoy 360-degree views from the tower.

OVERNIGHTING. A handful of lookouts remain unlocked and open for overnight stays on a first-come, first-served basis. Often these lookouts have a wooden bed platform, requiring that you bring a sleeping pad and sleeping bag. Some will have a few dishes, leftover stores of dry goods, books, or games—but never go to a lookout expecting any amenities beyond a roof and walls.

RENTING. Currently only two lookouts in this book (and in all of the Cascades) are available for overnight rental: Evergreen Mountain Lookout and Heybrook Lookout, both near Skykomish off US Highway 2, reserved through www.recreation.gov. Reservations must be made at least one day in advance and can be made up to six months in advance. Heybrook is typically available for rental starting in May, with the reservation window starting in November. Evergreen usually opens in late July, with reservations starting in late February or early March. Note that when the reservation window opens up, available dates book up quickly. Plan ahead and call local agencies about current conditions. Restorations are currently underway on North Mountain Lookout near Darrington to make it available for rental as well.

VOLUNTEER STAFFING. Several lookouts accept volunteers to staff the structures for a day or weekend at a time during the summer months. At these sites, volunteers are more of a backcountry presence and act as interpretive guides rather than actually fire watching. If you are interested, contact the ranger station listed. Six lookouts still

OPPOSITE *View of Kachess Lake and Mount Rainier from Thorp Mountain Lookout*

Bookshelf at Winchester Mountain Lookout

have full-season paid staffing, and the turnover tends to be low. Again, contact the ranger station for details.

This book covers all the lookouts in the Cascades and Olympics that are accessible on public land by at least a short walk. A list of other Washington lookouts still standing can be found in the appendix.

TIPS FOR A BETTER LOOKOUT EXPERIENCE

Keep these tips in mind as you plan your lookout adventures.

VISIT STAFFED LOOKOUTS DURING "BUSINESS" HOURS. Six of the lookouts covered in this book are still staffed in the summer. Try to visit only during business hours during fire season, usually 9:30 AM to 6:00 PM, when the staff radio in and out and are officially on the clock. Remember that this is someone's home—if the lookout staff don't see you right away, give a friendly shout and wait to be invited in.

BRING A SMALL GIFT. If lookout staff are on duty, consider bringing them a small gift of fresh fruit or a sweet treat. It's less imperative these days, as roads go closer to the summits and staff have days off, but back in the old days they would often be on-site for the whole summer with very limited supplies. If you were living in the woods for a week or month at a time, what "frontcountry" provisions would you appreciate? I love this story from Ira Spring and Byron Fish's *Lookouts* about staffer Barney Douglass who spent two summers on Desolation Peak and two on (the no-longer-standing lookout) Devils Dome.

He was away working on the trail when a couple of young women arrived at the lookout. In a burst of sympathy for the poor lonely man who lived there, they whipped up a batch of fudge for him. The fudge was good, Barney concedes, but he found they had used up his entire summer stock of chocolate and sugar.

RESPECT THE BUILDING. Never attempt to enter a catwalk if the trapdoor is locked, or attempt to enter a lookout cabin if the door is locked. If you see any signs of break-ins or vandalism, report it to the ranger station. If you see a boot brush outside the door of a lookout (such as at Evergreen or Winchester Mountain), use it before you walk inside. Lookout floors are often maintained through recaulking and repainting; the grit from the bottoms of shoes can shorten the life span of the work. Also remember that lookout structures come in wide-ranging states of repair, and some that are open to the public may be missing deck boards or have sketchy railings or broken glass in and around them. You're responsible for your own safety.

HAVE BACKUP PLANS FOR SLEEPING AND FOOD STORAGE. If you want to sleep in a lookout, always have a plan B in case it's already occupied. That entails a plan for where to camp and obtaining the appropriate permit, as well as plans for how to store your food. I have packed in a bear canister and then ended up sleeping in a lookout and not needing it—but always better to err on the side of caution.

BRING LAYERS. Did I mention how cold it can get up there? Do not underestimate how many layers you will need. I'm talking a hat, fleece or puffy jacket, gloves, thick socks, and a windproof shell.

LEFT *Boot brush at Evergreen Mountain Lookout* **RIGHT** *Catwalk in need of maintenance at Funk Mountain*

LEFT *Hardware remnant on trail to Mount Pilchuck* **RIGHT** *Saw on Lookout Mountain Lookout (Cascade River Road)*

CARRY A LOT OF WATER. Unfortunately, stunning mountain peaks and 360-degree views are often nowhere near good water sources. Just accept that you will have to carry a bit of water weight.

BE CATTLE-AWARE. Some lookouts, especially those located in the Okanogan National Forest, are on, or are surrounded by, grazing land,. Be aware of the potential for cattle on the roads, always leave gates as you found them, and never block a gate.

KEEP AN EYE OUT FOR LOOKOUT-RELATED HARDWARE REMNANTS. Discovering artifacts is an exciting aspect of visiting the lookout structures, many of which have been inhabited for nearly a century. On your lookout excursions, look for water storage, former cabin foundations, wire, bolts, etc., but always leave things where you found them.

BE FIRE-AWARE AND KEEP YOURSELF SAFE. This may seem obvious, but fire-lookout towers exist because, well, fires really happen. We have at least a few major forest fires each year, often very close to lookouts, as you will see for yourself on many hikes. Always check with the local ranger district before hiking to make sure the trail is open and safe.

....

Use extreme caution in recently burned areas, and even burns that are several years old. Note that burned forests aren't simply black—the trees may appear brown from a distance. The dead, standing burned trees are more likely to be unstable—listen closely for swaying trees and falling branches while hiking through them, especially in any kind of wind. Never camp beneath dead, burned trees.

The biggest fire effects you are likely to experience while hiking are seeing and smelling smoke and having your view obscured. Sometimes the air is still fairly clear, with a distinct pillar of smoke visible. But sometimes the whole horizon is hazy with whiteout conditions. Take care when navigating, as even distant fires can greatly limit visibility. And always remember that conditions can change quickly.

A burn in Glacier Peak Wilderness, visible from Miners Ridge

HOW TO USE THIS GUIDE

The lookouts in this guide are listed by their geographical locations, a primary consideration for many people when deciding on a hike. Maybe you want to do a day hike that's not too far from Seattle, or you're visiting friends near Olympia and want to explore farther south, or you're looking for a fun hike for your family on an outing to the Olympic Peninsula. The forty-four lookouts described are divided up into regions: the North, Central, and South Cascades and the Olympics. North is considered north of the Mountain Loop Highway, including the San Juans, Mount Baker Highway, State Route 20, the Methow Valley, and the Okanogan. Central includes hikes off US Highway 2 and Interstate 90. And the south region extends from State Route 410 and Mount Rainier south to the Oregon border. If you are more focused on a certain mileage or overall elevation gain, consult the at-a-glance chart immediately following the table of contents.

Each lookout listing starts with an information block of key hike details, beginning with **Year constructed**, which is the year that the current lookout was built, though it may be the second or third structure on that site.

Lookout access specifies how the public can interact with the structure—whether it's locked, open to the public for day visits, available for overnight stays, or still in use as an active lookout. If the lookout is still staffed, you may get to meet on-duty staff between late July and mid-September, otherwise a staffed cabin will be locked in the off-season.

Location tells you the land jurisdiction of the hike and the lookout. Most of Washington's remaining lookouts are on US Forest Service land in national forests, though a few are in national parks, state parks, or on Department of Natural Resources land. For sites managed by the USFS, the specific national forest is listed, as well as the relevant ranger district. In some cases, the local visitors center or office is listed.

Roundtrip distance is the total out-and-back distance, unless otherwise noted. A few hikes have options to vary the route length or to do a loop. Note that I have

OPPOSITE *Firefinder and the lookout staff's dog at Mount Leecher*

consulted maps and used my own GPS device to measure every route, but due to natural variances, the listed distances are not guaranteed to be exact.

Elevation gain is how many vertical feet you will ascend on the hike (rounded to the nearest ten). Some hiking books list this figure as a cumulative gain, which would include small elevation undulations in the trail. But in this book, because the vast majority of lookout hikes climb steadily upward, the elevation gain is listed as the simple gain—the difference between the trailhead elevation and the summit elevation.

Lookout elevations in this book range from 1700 to 7440 feet, with most lookouts being between 5000 and 7000 feet. While the lookouts are occasionally on ridges, the majority are on peak summits. As a rule of thumb, expect summits at 5000 feet or higher to have snow lingering until at least mid-July, if not later.

Mount Baker from trail to Park Butte

MAP LEGEND

(5)	Interstate highway		⊨	Bridge
(2)	US highway		▲	Campsite
(530)	State route		→	Direction of travel
1230	Forest road		🔭	Fire lookout
——	Main trail		⊢⊣	Gate
- - - - -	Alternate or loop trail		▲	Mountain or peak
∙∙∙∙∙∙∙	Other trail		❶	Parking
∙∙∙∙∙∙∙∙	Cross-country route		•	Point of interest
═══	Paved road		❶	Trailhead
▃▃▃▃	Gravel road		ⓣ	Alternate trailhead
- - - - -	Water taxi		▭	Park, forest, or wilderness area
⬬	Body of water		⸰⸰⸰	Meadow or marsh
—#—	Waterfall		⸦⸧	Glacier
——	River or stream			

Map recommends which maps (one of the Ten Essentials!) to bring with you. The maps you take hiking should be topographic maps that show three-dimensional relief with contour lines. Most of the hikes list Green Trails maps, which are based on standard 7.5-minute United States Geological Survey (USGS) maps. Other maps include actual 7.5-minute USGS maps, so named because they cover 7.5 minutes of longitude and 7.5 minutes of latitude. They are also defined by having a 1:24,000 scale, meaning 1 inch on the map represents 24,000 inches on the ground, equivalent to 2000 feet. This scale is very usable for navigation—zoomed out enough to give context to the surrounding area, but zoomed in enough to show meaningful detail.

GPS coordinates tells the Global Positioning System location of the trailhead. They are given in the format of degrees, minutes, and seconds using the WGS 84 datum.

Permits and fees lists regulations or required passes for parking at the trailhead, entering a wilderness area, or camping, if any. Many trailheads in national forests require either a Northwest Forest Pass (for Washington and Oregon use only) or an annual America the Beautiful Pass (good nationwide) displayed in your windshield in order to park. It's easiest—and ultimately less expensive if you visit these public lands at least a few times each year—to buy the annual pass (of either type) and just keep it in your car so you don't have to worry. America the Beautiful Passes cover several other agency-managed lands besides those managed by the US Forest Service and National Park Service, and there are several discount types for these passes as well. Without an annual pass, national parks often charge a per-car entry fee that is valid for seven consecutive days. The other pass listed in this book is the Discover Pass, required for state-owned lands such as state parks and Department of Natural Resources land. Other than parking or entry, you may need permits for overnight camping, especially in national parks. Often the permits are free or cost a nominal fee, but never skip them—they are essential to backcountry management and use data.

WHEN TO VISIT LOOKOUTS

Traditionally, all lookouts were staffed starting just before the snow had melted out, typically sometime in July, depending on the snowfall that year and the location. Lookout staff remained as long as there was fire danger, which was usually until sometime in September or possibly early October. So for snow-free, nontechnical hiking (what this book covers, with the exception of Three Fingers), that is a good timing guideline for you to follow as well: late July through late September. Of course, it varies by year, so always check current road and trail conditions with the local ranger district.

Some of the lookout hikes also work well as snowshoeing destinations and have good winter access routes. However, due to steep slopes and exposed approaches, most of the lookouts require technical mountaineering skills and avalanche safety training and knowledge to safely access them in the winter. Lookouts that are commonly accessible in winter are noted in individual descriptions.

1 MOUNT CONSTITUTION

YEAR CONSTRUCTED	LOOKOUT ACCESS		LOCATION
1938	Open to public		Moran State Park

Roundtrip distance: 6.6-mile loop (option of 6 or 7.2 miles out-and-back)
Elevation gain: 1490 feet
Lookout elevation: 2407 feet
Maps: USGS Mount Constitution; Moran State Park map published by Cascade Orienteering Club, for sale at local Eastsound bike shop
GPS coordinates: N 48° 39' 17" W 122° 10' 52"
Permits and fees: Discover Pass, or day-use self-registration at trailhead

GETTING TO THE TRAILHEAD

From the intersection of Crescent Beach Drive and Olga Road in Eastsound, turn right (south) onto Olga Road and drive southeast for 3.2 miles to the entrance of Moran State Park. Continue for an additional 1.3 miles and then turn left onto Mount Constitution Road. Follow it for 1 mile until the turn for Mountain Lake, and go right. Drive 0.2 mile to the parking area where the lake is on your right and a ranger house is on your left. The Mount Constitution Road is open year-round, except at times of heavy snowfall.

Getting to Orcas Island requires taking the San Juan Islands ferry from Anacortes. Reservations are always recommended for this Washington State Ferry route, and necessary during the summer (https://secureapps.wsdot.wa.gov/Ferries/). If you want to stay at any of the dozens of campsites at Moran State Park, reservations are required April 1 through October 31. Prime summer months are booked up to nine months in advance. Reserve online through the Washington State Parks website (https://washington.goingtocamp.com) or by calling 1-888-CAMP-OUT. Camping is on a first-come, first-served basis November through March, and sites usually have space available. The campsites on the east end of Cascade Lake are closest to the trailhead.

This forested hike in a state park takes hikers to the highest point in the San Juan Islands with a CCC-era watchtower and views of the upper Puget Sound. It makes for a great shoulder-season hike or winter snowshoeing trip.

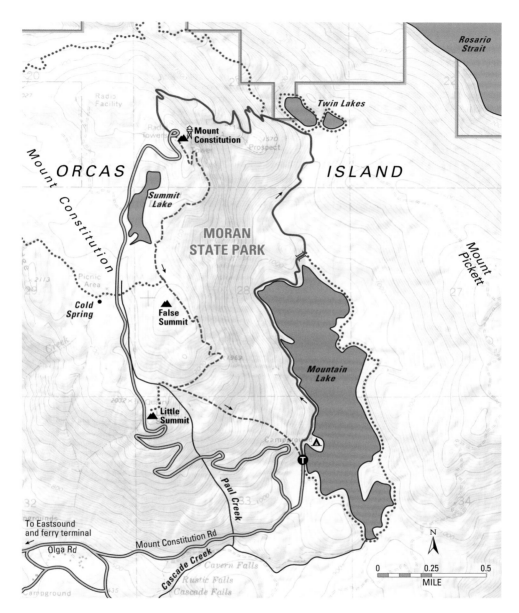

ON THE TRAIL

You can drive to the top of Mount Constitution, but where's the fun in that? This second-oldest state park in Washington has beautiful hiking trails with several options for reaching the summit. The route described below takes you up along the

A unique lookout: the stone tower at Mount Constitution

western edge of Mountain Lake and down by the eastern edge of Summit Lake. If you're looking for a shorter hike, you could opt for the out-and-back from the Summit Lake side of the loop instead, but the full loop has varied scenery, and the parts near Mountain Lake and Twin Lakes are lovely. These are also popular fishing lakes, if that's your thing; Mountain Lake has small kokanee and cutthroat trout, and the

Twin Lakes have eastern brook trout. Check regulations; both require licenses for individuals fifteen years old and older.

Start by walking 0.2 mile north on the same road you parked on to another parking lot. Stay to the left, following signs for "Mount Constitution Summit 3.4 mi." The trail begins wide along the western shore of Mountain Lake in a shady forest of hemlock, Oregon grape, salal, sword fern, and cedar.

At 0.7 mile, the trail moves slightly away from the water, and there is a knob of land on your right. If you walk up and over the knob (due east), you may find a rope swing at the lake's edge. Continue on as the trail begins to wrap around the north side of the lake. At 1.3 miles, you will cross a small bridge and reach a junction. Stay left (away from the lake), following signs for Twin Lakes. (If you have more time in the area, consider the full 4.2-mile trail around Mountain Lake, which continues to the right from here.) You are soon walking through a pretty meadow section with grasses and bracken fern on your left. By 2.1 miles, you reach the next junction. This is Twin Lakes, and staying right would put you on the figure-eight trail that winds between and around the two. It's a pretty spot and a worthy side journey if you have time.

To continue to the summit take a hard left (following signs for Mount Constitution) to leave the lake basin and start ascending. You will reach a junction with the trail to Cold Spring at 2.4 miles; stay straight. Now you're on a trail that is switchbacking up, mostly in shade, until 2.8 miles. As the trees thin, on a clear day you may be able to see Mount Baker to the east. By 3.4 miles, the trail flattens and gets wider, and by 3.5 miles it feels like you've gotten definitively higher. In about 150 feet, you'll reach the paved Mount Constitution Road leading into the Mount Constitution parking area.

Cross the road and follow another small patch of trail, then walk a few steps farther on the road, and you will see the back of the lookout tower up ahead. Follow the paved walking trail up (southeast) to the lookout, reaching it in 3.6 miles at 2407 feet of elevation. Do not let the relatively low elevation deceive you—the views are still phenomenal. In an island landscape, being two thousand feet above most other landforms—with unobstructed views—is pretty incredible. If you plan to spend a few days on Orcas Island, which you should, try to come here on the clearest day.

The summit area contains four picnic tables, a rocky sitting area, and a low stone wall at the edge of the viewpoint. Use caution near the edge, and you can peer over to see Twin Lakes and Mountain Lake way down below. (Pat yourself on the back!) Look south down Puget Sound and across to Bellingham. Mount Baker towers to the east, and if it's clear, you can see Mount Rainier to the south.

But this isn't even the full view yet! Head to the tower, a forty-five-foot stone observatory with a live-in top floor. As you walk up the interior staircase, the rooms on each level are packed with historical information and displays. At the top, display signs delineate

Hardware detail on the Mount Constitution tower

what you see on the horizon. You can go up a couple more steps to enter the small room and see the view to the north. Take in Sucia and Matia islands in the San Juan chain, and the mountains in Canada beyond. The only direction that you cannot see is west, as the tower and the trees block the views in that direction.

The displays share a fascinating history. Moran State Park is named after local naturalist Robert Moran, who donated the land in the 1920s for the public to enjoy and was named "Citizen of the Century" by San Juan County in 1989. Construction on the tower began in 1935 by the CCC, using one thousand tons of native sandstone quarried on the north side of Orcas Island. The CCC built fifty-five structures in the state park. The tower was in use until the 1960s, and it has been a scenic attraction since 1967. There are still around seventeen CCC-built structures in the park, including some of the kitchen shelters, restrooms, offices, storage sheds, and ranger residences. In the parking lot there is an original ranger cabin that is now a gift shop. At the summit there are restrooms and water, and someday there will be an interpretive center too.

The lookout is maintained by Friends of Moran, a nonprofit organization that raises money for state park projects. You can support them by volunteering or by donating money at the tower entrance; learn more about this group and all they have to offer at www.friendsofmoran.org.

Now you have a choice: return the way you came, or take a different way back by doing a loop. For the loop pick up the trail from the west side of the summit area, following signs for Little Summit—Cascade Lake—Cold Spring. Descend through the forest of lodgepole pines and thick salal undergrowth. The nice east-facing viewpoints continue for about three-quarters of a mile before you are back to just trees.

At 1 mile from the summit, you will reach a junction with signage; stay to the left, toward Little Summit, where the Department of Natural Resources operated a fire tower until the 1970s. Beginning at 1.4 miles, the trail descends more vigorously on switchbacks before flattening out a bit at 1.7 miles. You will reach another junction at 1.9 miles and turn left, onto the trail signed for Mountain Lake. Soon you'll be descending again, and the trail gets a bit rocky and rooty by 2.2 miles. After another half mile or so of steep descent, you'll see the road and know you're almost back to your car. At 2.8 miles, cross the footbridge near the road and stay on the trail, arriving at the parking lot at 3 miles from the summit.

2 WINCHESTER MOUNTAIN

YEAR CONSTRUCTED	LOOKOUT ACCESS	LOCATION
1935	Open to public for day visits	Mount Baker–Snoqualmie National Forest

Roundtrip distance: 3.4 miles
Elevation gain: 1300 feet
Lookout elevation: 6510 feet
Map: Green Trails Mt. Shuksan No. 14
GPS coordinates: N 48° 57' 9" W 121° 21' 51"
Permits and fees: Northwest Forest Pass to park; Glacier Public Service Center

GETTING TO THE TRAILHEAD

From the town of Glacier, drive east on State Route 542 for 12.5 miles. Turn left onto Forest Road 3065 (Twin Lakes Road), just after the Department of Transportation maintenance facility. The road is rocky and potholed, but drivable for the average passenger vehicle until the Yellow Aster Butte Trailhead at 4.5 miles. Park here if you have any reservations about your car making it the last 2.3 miles. From here, a high-clearance vehicle is essential, and four-wheel drive is helpful. The steep, narrow road is deeply rutted in places with a few sharp switchback turns. Vehicles frequently overheat on this steady climb, particularly on hot days. Pack your auto supplies, your best driving skills, and your patience for this drive. The road will level out by 6.4 miles and you'll pass campsites and a privy along the first lake. You will reach the trailhead where the road ends between the Twin Lakes at 6.8 miles from the turnoff

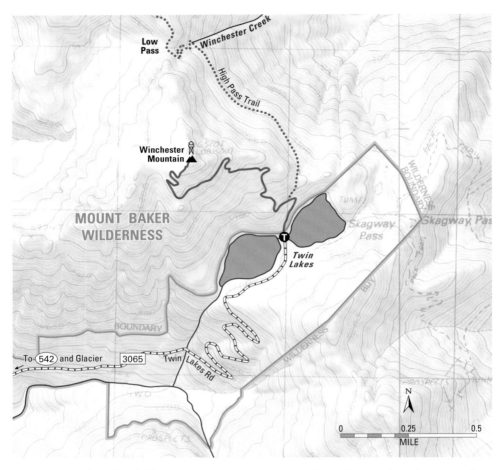

onto Twin Lakes Road. There are more campsites and another vault toilet, as well as ample parking.

> The trailhead alone is amazing, and a short, steep hike puts you deep into the Mount Baker Wilderness and a historic mining area with soaring North Cascades peaks all around.

ON THE TRAIL

Even though this hike is short, plan to take your time. It's a gnarly drive to the trailhead, but once you get there, it's so spectacular that you won't want to feel rushed. The pristine, manicured feel of the two lakes and designated campsites makes you wonder how you stumbled onto the quintessential subalpine car-camping site in the Pacific

Northwest. Take a few breaths to let your lungs adjust to the mile-high starting point, and let your eyes adjust to the sparkle of the turquoise waters of the Twin Lakes.

Feeling relaxed and rested? Good, because it's going to be a short-but-serious haul to the lookout. Pick up the trail at the north end of the parking lot between the two lakes. You will start climbing immediately up a sun-drenched, south-facing slope, wading through a jungle of green false hellebore. In summer, the trail is bursting with subalpine beauty—wildflowers like lupine, pink and yellow aster, and pink heather and sumptuous blueberries. After a quarter mile you reach the junction with High Pass Trail, where going right will take you farther afield to High Pass and Low Pass backcountry. Instead, stay to the left and keep climbing, enjoying the increasing expanse of flowers like lacy white cow parsnip, light pink (Miner's ridge) paintbrush plant, and Cascade azaleas.

Continue to switchback up. There is a section that gets pretty steep, and a step or two of scrambling. It feels like every 50 vertical feet the number of peaks you can see increases exponentially. It's astounding what a difference every bit of elevation makes.

At 6050 feet, enjoy a traverse—the trail is pretty narrow, but thankfully it's flattish and in decent shape. The traverse ends at a saddle at around 1.3 miles, where you will wrap around the western flank of the mountain and get wide views to the north and west.

This is the last bit! With just a few hundred more vertical feet to go, enjoy the new sights as you switchback upward. You'll see more peaks, squat subalpine evergreens,

Winchester Mountain Lookout

Western anemone and one of the Twin Lakes

and to the northwest, a small, permanent snowfield with views to Tomyhoi Lake beyond. After consistent switchbacks, the very last section is mostly red volcanic rock and more of a beeline to the summit.

You reach the lookout at 1.7 miles and 6510 feet. It's an L-4 ground house built in 1935, and it should be open to visitors in the summer. You can go inside and enjoy the lived-in feel—furnished with a creaky cot with foam pads, the firefinder stand, a long bench, and a chair. It's also stocked with batteries, sunscreen, a first-aid kit, maps, and books.

There is an open-air privy at the top, but it's been a bit overused. If you're up for it, consider packing out waste with a disposal kit.

The lookout was regularly staffed until 1966. It was forgotten for nearly two decades, but in the early 1980s the Mount Baker Hiking Club took over its maintenance. The club got a permit to restore and care for the structure, and you can find contact information inside, along with comics and old lookout photos (with history) hanging on the walls.

Even while inside the lookout, you are seemingly engulfed by an endless expanse of peaks. To the north you've got The Pleiades, Mount Larrabee, and American Border and Canadian Border peaks. Winchester is only 3 miles from the border! To the west is Yellow Aster Butte, and Mount Baker dominates the view to the southwest. Northwest is Tomyhoi Lake with Tomyhoi Peak beyond, and the view continues to Mount McGuire in Canada. To the south is Mount Shuksan, and to the east is Copper Mountain, the Picket Range, and Mount Redoubt.

How did hikers get access to this remote spot? The original pack trail was built in the early 1900s by miners who brought in supplies for a stamp mill at Lone Jack Mine and extracted $300,000 worth of gold. To get to the mine, the miners' trail continued beyond Twin Lakes to a saddle between Winchester and Goat mountains, a strenuous journey. The stamp mill was temporarily closed until accessibility improved. By the time a road was built, the mine and mill had fallen into ruins; however, even though the mining heyday was over, the road helped to make the area more accessible and popular for recreational use.

Return the way you came, taking extra care on the steep sections.

3 COPPER RIDGE

YEAR CONSTRUCTED	LOOKOUT ACCESS	LOCATION
1934	Closed to public; used as needed by National Park Service	North Cascades National Park, Mount Baker–Snoqualmie National Forest

Roundtrip distance: 19.4 miles
Elevation gain: 3200 feet (5300 feet cumulative; hike contains significant downhill sections)
Lookout elevation: 6260 feet
Maps: Green Trails Mt. Shuksan No. 14 and Mt. Challenger No. 15
GPS coordinates: N 48° 54' 36" W 121° 24' 30"
Permits and fees: Northwest Forest Pass required at trailhead; backcountry permit required for overnight stay in national park, available at Glacier Public Service Center

GETTING TO THE TRAILHEAD

From the Public Service Center in Glacier, drive 13 miles east on State Route 542. Turn left onto Hannegan Pass Road (Forest Road 32). At 1.3 miles, stay left, and then drive an additional 3.9 miles to the road's end. The trailhead is a large parking lot with a picnic shelter and privy. There are a few car-camping sites at Hannegan Campground just before you reach the trailhead.

Do this as an overnight or even a multiday trip, with a visit to the original 1930s lookout as one stop on the pristine Copper Ridge Loop deep in the North Cascades. Check with rangers about conditions as snow often lingers well into summer.

ON THE TRAIL

This one takes some extra planning, but is worth it. Getting to Copper Ridge (also called Copper Mountain) Lookout is best done as an overnight because of the roundtrip mileage—but permits are required and they go fast, especially on summer weekends. You can only get them a maximum of one day in advance, which can make planning difficult if the campsite you have in mind is not available. Camping at Hannegan Camp below Hannegan Pass does not require a permit (as it's in the national forest), but hiking to the lookout is still a haul from there. You could even consider doing the expedition to the lookout as part of the 34-mile Copper Ridge Loop Trail, a revered route that takes you high up onto the ridge and down to the Chilliwack River.

Start on the flat, shady trail with the sound of Ruth Creek below to your right and the Nooksack Ridge running along high above it. The vegetation is a mix of fireweed, ferns, and dogwood, along with thimbleberries, nettles, and goatsbeard. At about a quarter of a mile, you reach a small rockslide from 2016. Continue on, soaking in the beauty of this steep-sided valley with views of water cascading down the rock face across the river.

After 1.5 miles, the trail starts to steepen along the southwestern slope of Granite Mountain, with grand views up valley to snowcapped Ruth Mountain. Cross a small

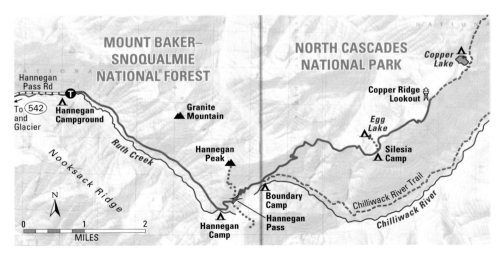

Copper Ridge Lookout with wildfire smoke obscuring the phenomenal view

creek around 2 miles. This stretch is mostly in the sun, so be prepared for a hot climb. At 3.5 miles, you reach the junction with Hannegan Camp. You want to stay left (north) but veering right takes you to a huge camping area, still in the national forest. There are no permits required to camp here, and there is a designated cooking area and privy. Just past the junction is a small creek and reliable water source should you need it.

Instead, stay left and continue the climb. At 4 miles you reach Hannegan Pass at 5082 feet. If you have the time and inclination, you could turn left (north) at the pass for a strenuous, scenic detour to Hannegan Peak, 1 mile each way and 1100 feet of elevation gain. But for the lookout, continue straight at the junction.

From here the trail drops downward, switchbacking steeply downhill for the next 0.7 mile, passing blueberries, until you reach the top of an open-bowl valley. At 4.8 miles, you reach a big rockslide and pick your way across the scree. This is prime terrain for bears and marmots, and for mountain goats up on the rocky bluffs across the way.

At 5 miles, you reach Boundary Camp at the national park boundary, where there are designated permit-required sites, a privy, and a metal bear box. Going right takes you down to the campsites and the junction for the Chilliwack River Trail—for those doing a loop. Stay left for the ridge, and you'll soon reenter forest and begin switchbacking up.

At 6.1 miles, and 5270 feet, views of Indian Mountain and Red Face appear to the east. At 6.2 miles, try to spot two insulators on a tree on your right. Immediately

View from trail to Copper Ridge

after that you'll cross a meadow of blueberries, grass, parsley, and false hellebore. To your right are views (due south and a little southeast and southwest), and to your left are big rock faces—also prime mountain goat terrain. There are more insulators in this area—white ones—and original wire at about 6.6 miles. Right after that, cross a scree slide-field washout where the trail is gravelly but in adequate shape. This section would be dangerous to cross in snow, however.

Views really start to open up around 6.8 miles and 5400 feet. By 7 miles, you have solidly reached the ridgeline, with views on both sides. This is the kind of hiking I live for—subalpine, dramatic, and expansive. From here to the lookout, take extra care to stay on the designated trails, avoiding walking on any vegetation, as there are areas closed for restoration. At 7.9 miles you reach the Silesia Camp junction to the right. At 8.2 miles you reach the Egg Lake junction to the left. As you can see, there are no shortages of stellar campsites—it's just a matter of snagging a permit in time.

Keep walking this absolute treasure of a North Cascades ridgeline for just over another 1.5 miles. You will reach the lookout at 9.7 miles and 6260 feet. (The precise high point of the ridge is just 20 vertical feet higher, a short walk north of the lookout.) This is the original L-4 ground house with a grange-hall roof built in 1934 by the US Forest Service. The lookout was transferred to the National Park Service in 1969 and has been in regular use. It is no longer staffed full-time, but Park Service employees are often on duty on weekends or as needed.

These days, it's used more as a patrol cabin than fire-spotting post. Wilderness rangers do backcountry inventory monitoring—checking permits, recording visitor numbers, monitoring garbage, and observing plane noise. They help with visitor safety and ensure that this corner of the Cascades stays as safe and pristine as possible. The building gets a major maintenance overhaul every ten years or so, with projects such as analyzing the siding for potential maintenance needs, replacing window panes, hanging a new door, and repainting the outside.

Staff get water by melting snow that usually lingers into late July on the ridge. After that, water must be carted from Copper Lake, approximately 1.5 miles farther down the trail.

To the south is Mineral Mountain, and to the southwest, gaze upon Ruth Mountain, Mount Shuksan, and Mount Baker.

From here, return the way you came if you are doing an out-and-back hike. Or to complete the Copper Ridge Loop, continue heading northeast toward Copper Lake, and the trail will meet back up with the main trail at Boundary Camp in approximately 19 miles.

4 PARK BUTTE

YEAR CONSTRUCTED	LOOKOUT ACCESS	LOCATION
1933	Open to public for day use; overnighting on a first-come, first-served basis	Mount Baker–Snoqualmie National Forest, Mount Baker Ranger District

Roundtrip distance: 7.5 miles
Elevation gain: 2190 feet
Lookout elevation: 5459 feet
Map: Green Trails Hamilton No. 45
GPS coordinates: N 48° 42' 25" W 121° 48' 45"
Permits and fees: Northwest Forest Pass to park

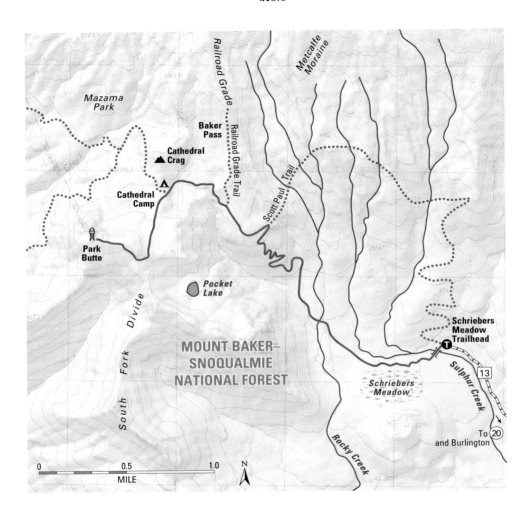

GETTING TO THE TRAILHEAD

From Burlington exit 230 on Interstate 5, head east on the North Cascades Highway (State Route 20) for 23 miles, turning left 0.4 mile after Milepost 82 onto Baker Lake Road. Continue 12.3 miles on Baker Lake Road. After crossing a bridge, turn left onto unmarked Forest Road 12. Continue 3.7 miles to the intersection with FR 13 and turn right. Proceed 5.3 miles to the end of the road at Schriebers Meadow Trailhead. There is a large parking area, but it's a popular trailhead, and if the lot is full you may have to park on the shoulder of the road on the way in. Privy available.

One of the most bang-for-your-buck lookout hikes consists of an easy drive from north-western Washington, a short hike, an open lookout, and stunning views up close and personal with Mount Baker.

ON THE TRAIL

Call it a flank, nubbin, knob, or outcropping—but no matter the name, this is a really cool spot on the south side of Mount Baker. Start at the Schriebers Meadow Trailhead. Depending on the time of year you're there, note other people's backpacks—this is a popular route for summiting Mount Baker, so you may see a lot of mountaineering gear. Wish them well and start hiking on the shady path with the gurgling of the river nearby. Cross a bridge over Sulphur Creek and the trail slopes upward very gently through hemlock, cedar, and fireweed. Pause in the dappled sunlight to snack on blueberries galore if the season is right.

Cross braidings of Rocky Creek at 1.1 miles, and again at 1.25 miles on a ladder bridge. Right after that, the trail gets a bit rocky and damp, like you are walking up a streambed. By 1.4 miles, cross the creekbed, and the trail gets more compact, heading upward more steadily. A bit of a switchback section is coming up.

At 2.1 miles and 4450 feet, you reach the junction with the Scott Paul Trail. Stay left for Park Butte and continue upward, luckily still mostly in the shade as you gain some elevation. Soon the forest canopy will thin, and heather will alert you to the subalpine Morovitz Meadow, with a big view of Mount Baker to your right.

Reflection of Mount Baker in tarn near trail to Park Butte

You'll see the junction for the Railroad Grade Trail to your right (north) at around 2.4 miles and 4680 feet. This is the point where mountaineers veer off to climb the mountain. You're looking directly at the Easton Glacier, where you may see climbers making their way up the slope.

You reach Cathedral Camp at 2.9 miles and 4840 feet. Hop off the main trail to your right (north) to find the four to five tent sites, some large stones that are nice for sitting and cooking, and a privy tucked in among the trees. This great campsite has views to the east and west. Bear canisters are not required for overnight stays, but I recommend using them anyway as I once saw a bear about half a mile before reaching Cathedral Camp. The trees at this site don't provide great options for bear hangs. They are tall but have thin, short, downward-sloping branches. Besides the big trees, this is a sweet little spot of heather, baby hemlocks, and cedars. There is also a lot of grass—in some places it's impossible to not walk on it, but where possible, do your best to stay on dirt trails and avoid trampling vegetation.

But back to the trail—we still have to get to the lookout! At the trail to Cathedral Camp, stay left (south), following the signed main trail. This last bit is a short, steep, really pretty ridge walk, with broader views every few minutes.

You reach the lookout at 3.75 miles. The L-4 ground house is nestled onto a tiny summit area among huge boulder slabs. There is not space to walk around the summit, but luckily you can stroll the wraparound catwalk. Take in the views from this amazing deck: the snow-clad majesty of Baker dominates the north. To the east are Mount Blum, Hagan Mountain, and Bacon Peak, with Baker Lake down below. Look west to the Twin Sisters and straight down the Middle Fork Nooksack River valley toward Puget Sound.

The lookout was built by the US Forest Service in 1933 and was in use until 1961. In September 1957, when the president of the Skagit Alpine Club visited Park Butte, he camped down in the meadow below. The lookout staffer hiked down to his camp and asked him to come up for the night for company, as he had not seen another person for thirty-nine days. That level of isolation is no longer the case, of course. This trail's short distance makes it very accessible and very popular; visit on a weekday or in the shoulder season if you can. Back in the 1970s when Mount Baker teased that it might erupt, the lookout also served as an observatory for volcano monitors. The Skagit Alpine Club now maintains the structure, and it's listed on the National Register of Historic Places.

Today you can go inside, sign the guest logbook, and read through a treasure trove of archived logs. There is also a bed platform, and the lookout is open for overnight stays on a first-come, first-served basis. Take in one last sweeping view and return the way you came.

OPPOSITE *Park Butte Lookout*

5 LOOKOUT MOUNTAIN (CASCADE RIVER ROAD)

YEAR CONSTRUCTED	LOOKOUT ACCESS	LOCATION
1962	Open to public for day use; overnighting on a first-come, first-served basis	Mount Baker–Snoqualmie National Forest, Mount Baker Ranger District; *side trip:* North Cascades National Park

Roundtrip distance: 9.4 miles

Elevation gain: 4480 feet

Lookout elevation: 5719 feet

Map: Green Trails Marblemount No. 47

GPS coordinates: N 48° 32' 14" W 121° 42' 20"

Permits and fees: None; side trip to camp at Monogram Lake requires a National Park Service backcountry permit, available at the Wilderness Information Center in Marblemount

GETTING TO THE TRAILHEAD

From State Route 20 in Marblemount, turn right onto Cascade River Road and immediately cross a bridge over the Skagit River. Continue for 7.1 miles to the trailhead on the right side of the road, with space for approximately twelve cars.

This relentless climb into the heart of the breathtakingly beautiful North Cascades is more than worth it—a lookout tower open for overnights and a possible lake side trip.

ON THE TRAIL

Apologize to your quadriceps in advance, because you will get no mercy from this trail. Climbing begins immediately from the north side of Cascade River Road, with the rush of the river loud and close. Heed the signboard that you will reach shortly up the trail, with a trail register, updates on recent wildlife activity, and the recommendation that only one or two people stroll on the lookout's catwalk at a time. The trail switchbacks up and up through a forest of hemlock, cedar, sword fern, vine maple, thimbleberry, Oregon grape, and salal.

It's a good thing you're in the shade, because you're going to be sweating. In the first mile, you ascend 1090 feet! Don't forget to take breaks—drink water and recalibrate your layers. At 1.75 miles, you will emerge from the towering evergreens into a sunnier section of midsized alder and maple. The trail becomes lush and

Lookout Mountain Lookout on a flower-filled summit

overgrown with salmonberry, green false hellebore, and bracken fern. If it happens to be wet—with dew or recent rain—you'll be soaking wet. Keep your eye out for prickly devil's club and nettles crowding the trail. By 2 miles, you exit this jungly

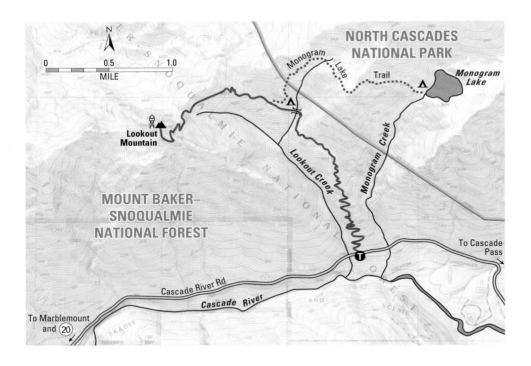

section and head back into forest. You've also ascended more than 2200 feet, and luckily will now get a short flat bit. At 2.4 miles, cross a bridge over a creek, a tributary of the nearby Lookout Creek, a good spot to get water if needed. In a few hundred feet, you'll cross the creek again and pass a couple campsites—no permits needed in the national forest.

At 2.7 miles, you reach the junction with the Monogram Lake Trail. If you have time, this is a highly worthy side trip. It may be ambitious to try to get to both the lake and the lookout in the same day (which are nearly equidistant from this junction), but it's an option, as is spending an additional night. If time permits, have fun with the possibilities for a stellar itinerary. If you want to venture to Monogram Lake, take the trail spur to the right (east) and follow it for 2 miles. Don't be fooled into thinking "side trip" means less climbing. There is still a lot of elevation gain in this direction—up to a stunning ridgeline before descending into a bowl that cradles the beautiful alpine lake, with designated camping and jaw-dropping views.

But let's keep going to the lookout. At the junction, continue straight (northwest). You'll cross a stream again at 2.9 miles, and if you plan to stay at the lookout, you should probably top off your water here, as it's your last reliable source.

At around 4640 feet, you'll reach a bit of a clearing and get your first view of the lookout on the cliffside above. It seems like it's not that far away, but you still have well over 1 mile to go. Luckily the grade mellows, and you get to enjoy a pretty traverse through the lush meadow until 3.8 miles, when you start switchbacking up. Note that while well defined, the path is narrow and requires some focus to keep your footing. The view south continually opens up, and you can spot Snowking Mountain in Glacier Peak Wilderness.

Finally, at 4.5 miles, the trail swings hard back to the west, and suddenly you can see over the other side of the ridge you've been scaling. You are almost there—one last little stretch up the ridgeline. There is an open-air privy tucked in among the trees on the southeastern side of the summit area. The lookout looms ahead to the north as you cross the flattish, grassy hilltop, dotted with lupine and aster, with views both east and west. You reach the lookout tower at 4.7 miles and 5719 feet.

Climb the 38 steps up to the wraparound catwalk and soak in the expansive view. Your big effort has garnered big rewards. Look southeast down the Cascade River valley and west to the Skagit River valley. Marblemount is directly below, but is blocked by a shoulder of the summit area. To the northwest is Bacon Peak, with Mount Shuksan and Mount Baker beyond. The cluster of the Picket Range is due north. To the northeast is Teebone Ridge with Big Devil and Little Devil peaks and Snowfield Peak beyond. Feast your eyes on glaciated mountains to the east, including Eldorado

Sunset mountainscape reflection in the windows of Lookout Mountain Lookout

and the plethora of Boston Basin glaciers. You can see the Hidden Lake Peaks to the southeast before Cascade Pass, but the Hidden Lake Lookout (a sister lookout) is too small to be seen easily with the naked eye unless you know exactly where to look.

Inside you'll find two bed platforms, the firefinder stand with the original tracks (but no firefinder), books, dishes, and guest logbooks. An especially cool feature? The outside cold box that is accessed through the floor in the lower cupboard in the northwest corner of the building. The lookout is open on a first-come, first-served basis to overnight visitors. Consider making a donation or sending comments via the preaddressed donation envelopes.

Built on this site in 1929, the first structure was a cabin with a gigantic dog-house-type appendage placed on top as a cupola. The construction was somewhat haphazard, and there was not a lot of confidence in the structure standing the test of time. The thirty-foot tower you see today was built in 1962, and by contrast, is a sturdy, modern fifteen-foot-by-fifteen-foot R-6 flat-roofed lookout. Whereas its predecessor's building materials were brought in by mule, these were mostly flown in by helicopter. The two lookouts stood side by side for five years, until the original was torn down in 1967. Maintenance work was done on the building in 1995, and it's currently cared for by a couple of individuals who live in Bellingham. The structure is now on the National Register of Historic Places.

Return the way you came.

6 HIDDEN LAKE

YEAR CONSTRUCTED	LOOKOUT ACCESS	LOCATION
1931	Open to public for day and overnight use	Mount Baker–Snoqualmie National Forest; Hidden Lake in North Cascades National Park, Mount Baker Ranger District

Roundtrip distance: 8 miles

Elevation gain: 3280 feet

Lookout elevation: 6890 feet

Maps: Green Trails Diablo Dam No. 48 and Cascade Pass No. 80

GPS coordinates: N 48° 30' 51" W 121° 46' 42"

Permits and fees: None; free backcountry permit required from National Park Service to camp at Hidden Lake, available at Wilderness Information Center in Marblemount

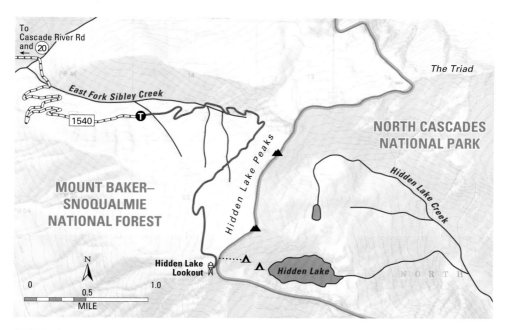

GETTING TO THE TRAILHEAD

From Marblemount on State Route 20, drive the Cascade River Road for 9.7 miles. Turn left onto Forest Road 1540, signed for Hidden Lake. The road is steep and rutted, though it is usually suitable for low-clearance vehicles if you go slowly and use caution. Washouts are common on this road—check current conditions with the ranger district before going. Follow FR 1540 for 4.7 miles until it ends at the trailhead.

> Wow. Any rumors you've heard about Hidden Lake Lookout being a gem are not overblown. In just 4 miles, you'll seemingly be floating in the middle of all the peaks of the North Cascades. If you go later in summer, you have a better chance of avoiding a sometimes year-round snow gully.

ON THE TRAIL

This is a fairly short hike, but that doesn't mean easy. Be extra prepared—I recommend shoes with good tread, trekking poles, the higher end of your water carrying capacity, and layers suitable for both very hot and very cold weather.

Start on the shady, rocky trail, walking east from the parking lot. You'll be alongside a small creek for the first 0.25 mile. Then the trail starts switchbacking upward through cedar and hemlock, with native trailing blackberry and swaths of deer, lady,

North Cascades view from inside Hidden Lake Lookout

and maidenhair ferns dotting the sides of the trail. If the season is right, you can graze on blueberries before reaching wooden stairs at 0.7 mile, and then a boardwalk that lasts for a tenth of a mile or so.

Soon after, by 0.9 mile, you emerge from the trees and get a view of huge, rocky pinnacles ahead—and the open slopes below, where you are headed. The tall evergreen trees have disappeared, and you are in a lush river valley. You'll feel dwarfed by the verdant slide alder, Pacific red elderberry, and huge bracken fern.

Cross East Fork Sibley Creek at 1 mile (a narrow creek without a footbridge), and refill water if you need to—this is the last reliable spot for a while. You've gone up a respectable 850 feet so far, and that was all in the shade. The next mile is going to be a push, going up over 1000 vertical feet. The trail switchbacks constantly on this grassy slope, the flies are known to be relentless in summer, and the path is narrow, south facing, and shadeless. Look up and to the right (east) to see the brightly colored, moving dots that are other hikers and get a sense of where you are going.

It's a beautiful subalpine slope, with thistle, pink aster, fireweed, and thimbleberry. Keep an eye out for the jagged leaves of stinging nettles appearing around

1.25 miles. You keep getting more and more views to the west as you gain elevation, and by 1.75 miles you will be able to see Mount Baker to the northwest. At 2 miles, you recross the same creek you crossed at 1 mile—but here at 5400 feet it's a dry creekbed in summer.

Now you get a little reprieve as the trail trends southwesterly on more of a traverse through meadows and heather. By 2.2 miles you reach your first rock field of large, white boulders as you keep going up, and the views grow to the north and west. This next 1 mile takes you up another 700 feet. At 3.2 miles, the lookout comes into view in the distance, and it seems to be balanced on an impossible perch set on a maze of boulders and snow. Listen for water; around this point on the trail snow may linger year-round, and there is often a water source from snowmelt on the left (east) side of the trail. This is also prime pika habitat; listen for those little guys cheeping as well. You are still in the national forest, and there are a couple places to camp after the 3-mile mark.

Continue on, as the trail gets rockier with many varying paths. Try to always take the gentler, rockier sections, as the other paths you see may show more exposed soil and are often unofficial cuts to the trail; walking on these perpetuates denuding of the vegetation. At 3.6 miles, pay close attention to your map. There is a short section where you are heading due east, but the trail may be covered by a year-round snow gully. If you go later in summer, you are more likely to avoid snow, since it will have had more time to melt out. Watch for bootpack, cairns, and rock scrambling options, and do whatever you are most comfortable with to get through this area.

At 3.7 miles, you reach the saddle at 6618 feet. This is the national park boundary and junction to Hidden Lake or the lookout. Take a moment to gawk at this amazing vantage point. Dropping down into the big bowl to the east would take you to the sparkling waters of Hidden Lake and designated camping—permit required as this is the national park and there is a limit on overnight visitors. From the saddle, it looks like a big boulder field, but there are flat spots interspersed on the slope and in the designated-camping areas.

To reach the lookout, head south to start up the switchback of the eastern slope of the Hidden Lake peak that the lookout is on, staying in the national forest. You can't see the lookout at the moment, but you're getting really close. The trail is fairly well defined, but narrow and screelike in places, and may be a challenge for beginning hikers. Take your time and watch your step.

By 3.9 miles, the trail disappears as you reach the ridgeline, and the summit turns into a pile of boulders. Keep your eye out for bits of trail and stacks of rocks and just keep going upward. Finally, the lookout appears ahead, and you may have to scramble a little bit on the boulders before reaching the building at 4 miles and 6890 feet.

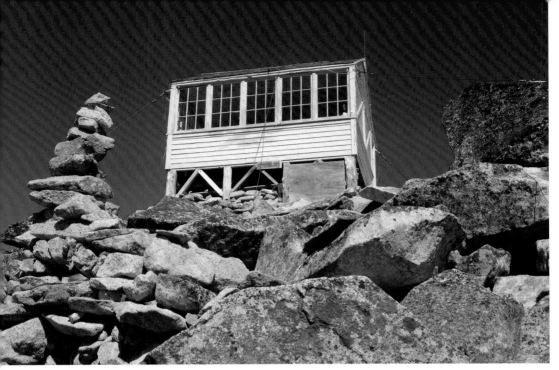

Hidden Lake Lookout

Where to start first—inside or outside? They both have so much to offer. The inside of the 1931 L-4 cab is cozy with its cabinlike furnishings. There is a double bed surface, a desk, counters, and mugs hanging up. This is one of the only lookouts where the firefinder stand is no longer there—but its absence creates more open space for visitors and overnight options. The woodstove is another traditional furnishing that was also removed in recent years, and you can see the circular patch in the ceiling where the stovepipe used to go.

The lookout was used for fire spotting until 1953. A husband-and-wife team staffed the lookout that season, and they recalled a four- to six-inch snowfall in August. The lookout was abandoned until 1961, when a casual group formed as Friends of Hidden Lake Lookout and took over the maintenance. It's been open to the public since then, giving it the unique status of having a longer life as a mountaintop hut than as an active lookout. It was added to the National Register of Historic Places in 1987. The man who spearheaded the group did so until the late 1990s, and passed away in 2007, but the Friends have continued the maintenance effort since then.

Now, back outside to the 360-degree view into the heart of the Cascades. With a view to Cascade Pass, this was the US Forest Service's eastern outpost up the Cascade River. Looking east beyond Hidden Lake is Buckner Mountain, Storm King, Johannesburg Mountain, Mount Torment, Sahale Mountain, Boston and Forbidden peaks. You can also see The Triad and Eldorado and Klawatti peaks to the northeast.

To the north are Snowfield and Colonial peaks. Mounts Baker and Shuksan are to the northwest. Snowking Mountain, LeConte Glacier, and Mount Formidable are closer to the south, with majestic Glacier Peak in the distance. It's a similar view to what you would see from the lovely Lookout Mountain (Hike 5), but a handful of miles closer to the Cascade Crest and nearly 1200 feet higher.

The building is available for overnight stays on a first-come, first-served basis. It's a tremendous privilege that the lookout is still open to the public, but it is at risk of being loved to death. It's extremely popular, and not all visitors are as conscientious as you, dear reader. Please heed all the guidelines posted in the building: use extreme caution with fire around this old wooden building; cook outside if weather allows and inside use the provided Coleman shell under your stove; and do not use candles. Do not raise the fragile shutters, and do not go in the attic.

In addition, the current, unflagging Friends of Hidden Lake volunteer who has been coordinating the maintenance efforts for the past ten years urges visitors to remember to take care of the lookout by not leaving trash or broken bottles, and also to be self-sufficient and bring everything you need. Don't assume that something will be at the lookout or that you'll have access to it. There is a privy, but it is getting full and needs maintenance. If you're up for it, bring a human waste disposal kit to minimize your impact. Finally, if you want to stay overnight, don't plan to turn away other overnight hopefuls if you get there first. It's a public place that many people want to experience,

Switchbacking trail to Hidden Lake Lookout with view of Mount Baker

and it's best if that experience can be shared. Consider donating what you can, with a suggested $15 to $25 per night to help cover maintenance expenses. There are always maintenance needs on such an old building in such a harsh environment, and extreme measures are needed to accomplish them. For instance, when the roof was repaired in August 2016, materials had to be flown in by helicopter.

Inside the lookout you will find more information about the Friends of Hidden Lake Lookout: how to contact them, make a donation, report a maintenance issue, volunteer, or just learn more about how to support their efforts.

Return the way you came, taking extra caution going down the 0.5 mile below the summit.

7 SOURDOUGH MOUNTAIN

YEAR CONSTRUCTED	LOOKOUT ACCESS	LOCATION
1933	Closed to public; staffed as needed	North Cascades National Park

Roundtrip distance: 10.6 miles
Elevation gain: 5090 feet
Lookout elevation: 5985 feet
Map: Green Trails Diablo Dam No. 48
GPS coordinates: N 48° 43' 04" W 121° 51' 15"
Permits and fees: None; permits required for camping, available at Wilderness Information Center in Marblemount

GETTING TO THE TRAILHEAD
From Marblemount, drive east on State Route 20 for 20 miles. Turn left on Diablo Road and proceed 0.7 mile, passing Gorge Lake Campground on your right. Cross the Stetattle Creek bridge, bear right and arrive at the trailhead in 0.25 mile.

With more than 5000 feet of gain, this is one of the most vertical, quad-burning hikes to a lookout in Washington. If that weren't enough, it is also the site for one of the first lookouts in the United States, and was staffed for a summer by writer Gary Snyder. The main trail begins in the town of Diablo, but the lookout is also accessible via Pierce Mountain Way, a trail from Ross Lake.

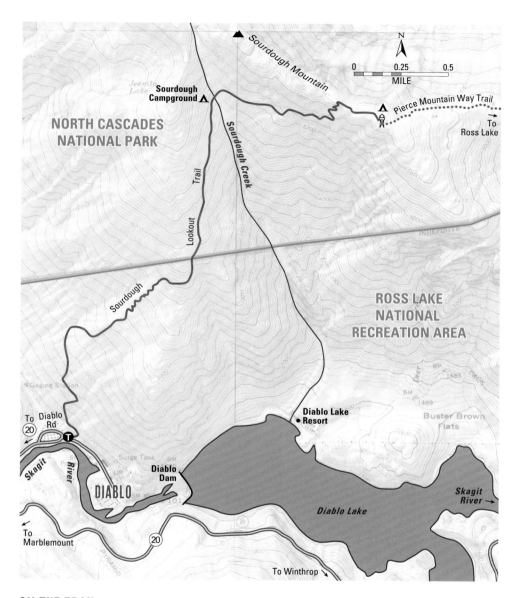

ON THE TRAIL

The lookout is visible from State Route 20, but until you know where to look, it might be hard to spot the tiny dot way up on the ridge. The trailhead is below 900 feet—but don't worry, the trail takes you high in a hurry. It starts in the town of Diablo, right by the Skagit River where it comes out of Diablo Lake. Follow the narrow trail up and up on switchbacks through the shady forest.

At just over 2 miles, you gain views down to SR 20, Diablo, and some surrounding peaks. By 3 miles the switchbacks stop, and you reach a bit of a clearing. You'll start seeing the white rocks of Sourdough Creek to your right. When you reach 4975 feet, you can cross the creekbed, which may or may not have water in it, depending on the time of year. To the left, before crossing, you'll see the junction to Sourdough Campground, which has a couple of campsites and a toilet. Permits are required and can be obtained in person at the ranger station in Marblemount.

After crossing the creek, the trail narrows considerably. Continue on for about a half mile in the woods and notice the views as they really start opening up around 5600 feet. The trail gets rockier before another series of switchbacks. Finally, at 4.7 miles and 5860 feet, you reach the ridge on Sourdough Mountain and can see down the other side toward Ross Lake. You've suddenly appeared on an alpine knoll with huge boulders and dainty heather—take care to stay on the path to protect the vegetation. This ridgeline becomes stunning as you make your way toward the lookout, a bit farther on. There are two campsites and a privy in the meadows just below the lookout.

At 5.3 miles and 5985 feet, you will arrive at the site of one of the first lookouts in the United States, a cupola from 1917. How did this spot way up in the North Cascades not only get discovered, but get trodden enough to become a lookout site?

Let's go back a generation earlier, to the 1890s. A woman named Lucinda Davis came to the upper Skagit River area from Colorado as a single mom with three kids. She turned an old cabin into a roadhouse and store for the local miners. When her son Glee was a boy, they would take horses up the south side of Sourdough Mountain, carving out the early trail—seems like a lot of work for a picnic! They began stacking cairns on the flattish site of the current lookout around the turn of the century.

In 1916, Glee Davis started working for the US Forest Service. When asked to scout a location for the area's first fire lookout, he naturally thought of Sourdough. After more than a decade of establishing the trail as a labor of love, his first paid task was to string six miles of telephone line to the false summit, which would be the location of a temporary lookout tent, while a cupola-style lookout was built on the present site.

Glee's 1917 cupola was replaced in 1933 by the L-4 cabin you see today, on what was then Mount Baker National Forest land. It was transferred to the National Park Service when the North Cascades National Park was created by Congress in 1967. The lookout is listed on the National Historic Lookout Register and is staffed on an as-needed basis during the summer by the Park Service.

North Cascades view from Sourdough Lookout Trail

A famous era in Sourdough's history was when poet and author Gary Snyder staffed the lookout here. Though based in California, Snyder worked a couple summers in Washington in the 1950s. In 1952, he requested to be placed in the most remote and difficult-to-access location and was sent to Crater Mountain, just east of Sourdough (and which no longer has a lookout on it). When Snyder returned to the Diablo guard station in 1953, he was assigned to Sourdough Mountain.

Even then, it probably had a similar remote-but-accessible feel. The Diablo Dam had been built and was generating power for Seattle by the 1930s, and Seattle City Light offered tours of the dam to promote hydroelectricity. Every week, thousands of people took the train from Seattle to Diablo. The tours dropped off during World War II and picked back up slightly afterward, making the area more of a tourist destination than it would have been otherwise.

Even though it's a haul, you'll thank the Davis family for sharing one of the best picnic spots ever. To be able to truly enjoy your snack and the view, however, you'll want to bundle up—the wind is bitterly cold when it's blowing from the north.

The closest peak to the west is Davis Peak. It was originally called Stetattle Peak, but as it became associated with Lucinda Davis and her family, it was eventually renamed. Beyond Davis Peak and slightly to the north are the darkly named points

Sourdough Mountain Lookout

of the Picket Range: Mounts Fury, Challenger, Terror, and Despair. And even farther north is Mount Redoubt. East of Sourdough Mountain and sprawling northward is the long arm of Ross Lake spreading up past the US-Canada border. Up to the northeast are Desolation Peak and Hozomeen Mountain, and east of the lake are Jack Mountain and Crater Mountain. Looking southeast you've got Ruby Mountain and Mount Logan. Due south down below are the sparkling turquoise waters of Diablo Lake and the glaciated masses of Colonial and Snowfield peaks beyond.

Continuing east from the lookout would put you on the Pierce Mountain Way Trail toward Ross Lake, which is another, less traveled, approach to Sourdough. Return the way you came, watching your step (and tired quads) on the steep descent.

8 DESOLATION PEAK

YEAR CONSTRUCTED	LOOKOUT ACCESS	LOCATION
1932	None; full-time resident staff in summer—locked when not staffed	North Cascades National Park, Ross Lake National Recreation Area

Roundtrip distance: 45.2 miles

Elevation gain: 4400 feet

Lookout elevation: 6102 feet

Maps: Green Trails Mt. Logan No. 49, Diablo Dam No. 48, and Ross Lake No. 16

GPS coordinates: N 48° 42' 29" W 120° 01' 18"

Permits and fees: None; free backcountry permit required for overnight stay in national park

GETTING TO THE TRAILHEAD

There are two quite different routes to reach this lookout. You can either hike in the entire way or arrive via boat and then hike from Ross Lake Resort.

From State Route 20 in Marblemount drive to the East Bank Trailhead, located 0.3 mile east of Milepost 138 on the north side of the highway. Hike north along the East Bank Trail for 16 miles to Lightning Creek Campground. The Desolation Peak Trailhead originates at the campground.

If you prefer an option that involves less hiking and a boat ride, from SR 20 drive to the Ross Lake/Dam Trailhead near Milepost 134. Hike north along the Ross Lake Dam Trail for 0.8 mile, until you reach a gravel road. Turn right (east) onto the gravel road, and follow it for approximately 0.45 mile until it ends at a boat dock. There is a phone 0.1 mile from the end of the road. Use the phone to contact Ross Lake Resort for pickup. The pickup ride to the resort takes a few minutes, with a nominal per-person fee. From there, you can rent a motorboat, canoe, or kayak from the resort, or take the Ross Lake Resort water taxi. (As of 2017, canoe and kayak rentals ranged from $40 to $112 for up to two people per day; motorboat rental was $125 per day for up to five people; and the taxi service was a flat $130 each way for up to six passengers.) Reservations should be made in advance for any boat option, as equipment and services are often booked ahead in summer, especially on weekends; contact Ross Lake Resort for more information.

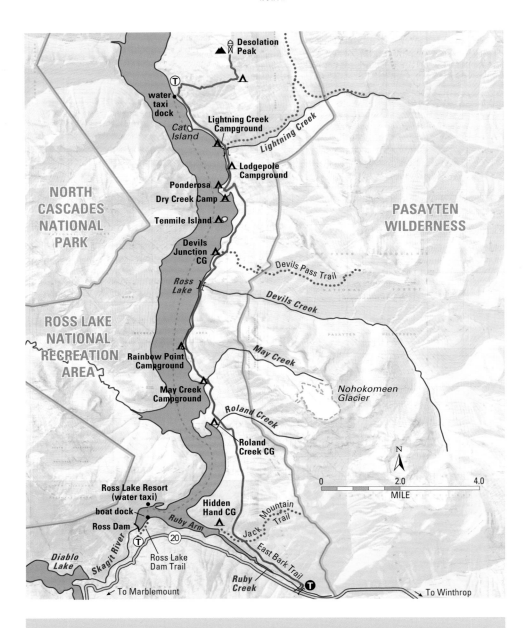

One of Washington's most remote lookouts has literary significance to boot. Tucked between jagged peaks in the North Cascades National Park, it offers views to the long sprawl of Ross Lake below. The journey is a long, multiday backpack—unless you want to shave miles off by taking a boat on the lake.

Hozomeen Mountain from Desolation Peak

> *And it was all mine, not another human pair of eyes in the world were*
> *looking at this immense cycloramic universe of matter. I had a tremen-*
> *dous sensation of its dreamlikeness which never left me all that summer*
> *and in fact grew and grew . . .*
>
> —*Jack Kerouac,* The Dharma Bums

ON THE TRAIL

Getting to the fire lookout on Desolation Peak is not for the faint of heart. It presents more logistical considerations than almost any other hike in this book. But it is flat-out spectacular. Desolation Peak Lookout is best known as the place writer Jack Kerouac lived and worked in the summer of 1956, and wrote about in his novels *The Dharma Bums* and *Desolation Angels*. The characters and stories are fictionalized but based on his autobiographical experiences.

Apart from the literary history, Desolation Peak is unusual because it can be reached by two different access points. Neither option is simple, but that only adds to the reward of the journey. You must either hike in 16 miles or take a somewhat expensive boat ride of 13 miles to reach the trailhead on the eastern shore of Ross Lake (details in Getting to the Trailhead).

Assuming that most people will opt for the full overland hike, I present the boating option as an alternative. It's a fabulous backpack because there are so many campsites

Desolation Peak Lookout

to choose from all along the trail, and you get gentle, forested trail, lakeside fun, and a mountain assault all in one hike. The campsites along the lake have designated tent sites, toilets, water access, picnic tables, and metal bear boxes. If you are not camping at the lakeside sites that have bear boxes, you will need to bring a bear canister.

Start at the East Bank Trailhead, where you will head slightly downhill to Ruby Creek. Cross the bridge and turn left, following the sign for "East Bank Trail 2.7." This is a nice, rolling section of trail along the creek, basically covering the miles to get over to Ross Lake. You'll pass vine maple, fir, huckleberry, Oregon grape, bracken fern, sword fern, alder, and moss trailside.

As promised, at around 2.7 miles, follow the (signed) trail to the right for the East Bank Trail. The scene changes from a leafy creekside corridor to a more evergreen forested one with several creek crossings. At 6.5 miles, pass Roland Creek, where there is also a campsite, and you'll finally start to see the lake to your left.

At a little over 7.5 miles, you reach May Creek Campground right on the creek; cross the river on a big log. The next camp area is Rainbow Point, with campsites off to the left and a bit of shore. If you feel like swimming, this might be a good spot—even though the trail goes right along the lake, you are a bit above the water most of the time, making water access more difficult than you'd think.

Cross a big bridge at Devils Creek, before reaching Devils Junction Campground. Going to the right at this junction takes you to Devils Pass, but you want to continue straight toward Hozomeen Mountain. Cross another log bridge, and then switchback upward a few times before reaching Lodgepole Campground.

Next is the Lightning Creek footbridge at your 16-mile mark. After you cross, stay right, following the sign to Hozomeen. Shortly after that, you reach another junction, and this time stay left, following the sign to Desolation. You'll climb upward, above the water, and in another mile or so reach an open point—a beautiful grassy knoll with a view down to the lake and Cat Island directly west of you.

Continue on until you reach the Desolation Peak Trailhead junction at 18 miles. If you were to turn left at this junction, it would take you down to the lakeshore and a dock in 0.15 mile, which is the waterside trailhead for Desolation if you were to come or go by boat from Ross Lake Resort. (There is a privy there, if you need one. It's also a short, worthwhile side trip if you want to fill up on water or hang out on or swim from the floating dock.) From this junction at 1800 feet, go right (northeast) to begin the immediate climb up the western slope of Desolation Peak.

The trail starts switchbacking upward through the shady forest of Douglas fir and alder, crossing several streams. It's a serious climb—you'll ascend just over 1000 feet in the first mile. At 19.9 miles there is a potential water source (usually still trickling in later summer), and definitely your last. Fill up on water here if needed, as the climb will continue to be dry and steep. At 20.5 miles, you will have gone up more than 2000 feet since the trailhead junction, and the forest begins to thin and open a bit. You emerge into an exposed traverse. It's a trade-off—you are now in the sun, but the view is expansive as you peer down to the lake and surrounding peaks. By 20.7 miles the views are bigger as you traipse through spirea, ferns, and thimbleberry. Continue your ascent on the rocky slope, greeted by the sounds of nearby pika. Watch for bears and marmots as well.

At 21.5 miles, you reach the junction for the camping area, and the trail will flatten slightly. You have to plan ahead to camp here though—a permit is required and only one party per night may camp here. You must stop at the Wilderness Information Center at the Marblemount Ranger Station to obtain the permit for an overnight stay. The campsite is to the right, but you are staying left for the last mile to reach the summit. Enjoy a little shade again, graze on blueberries, and pick your way over some rocky patches as you go up the last 950-foot vertical push to the lookout, with views expanding seemingly every few steps. High up here, it's also likely that you'll encounter patches of snow into late summer.

Ross Lake, Jack Mountain, and beyond from the trail to Desolation Peak

The terrain gets drier and more alpine, with subalpine fir and grassy knolls. You'll catch your first view of the lookout at 21.9 miles. It seems high above you, but you're almost there! Push on a little farther to reach the wide, flat summit area surrounded by sloping meadows, and arrive at the lookout at 22.6 miles and 6102 feet.

Desolation Peak was first climbed in 1926, the same year that a large fire laid waste to its slopes—hence the name Desolation. This is the original fourteen-by-fourteen-foot ground house from 1932. The peak was part of the Mount Baker National Forest before it was transferred to the National Park Service in the late 1960s. The lookout is staffed in summer, but if there is not an on-duty staff member there, the structure will be locked. In summer the shutters will be open, and you can see inside to the gas appliances (fridge, stove, and oven), desk, counter, bed, bookshelf, and the firefinder in the middle of the room. Don't miss the chance to sign the logbook outside the door. Not only is this one of the farthest-back, hardest-to-reach lookouts in Washington State, it is one of the most remote active lookouts in the nation. Regarding the really remote lookouts like Desolation, Ira Spring and Byron Fish wrote in *Lookouts*:

> *Whatever supplies lookout personnel needed for the summer had to be planned for the first and only packtrip. If they ran out of anything, all*

they could do was call in to the ranger station in the faint hope that some-one might have business up their way and bring it along.

....

No doubt a place this wild forces residents to take a good stock of basic needs—food, firewood, and other supplies to remain comfortable in any weather that may be thrown at them. Early in summer, when the main character in Kerouac's *The Dharma Bums* (based on Kerouac himself) first arrived at the summit on a gray day, Kerouac writes: "I gulped. It was too dark and dismal to like it. 'This will be my home and rest-ing place all summer?'" But if you go on a nice day later in the summer, you likely won't have that experience at all. The flowers will be colorful, the peaks, awe-inspiring, and the lake, sparkling.

Check out the summit area, but take care to stay on footpaths to avoid walking on fragile vegetation. There is a composting toilet on the east side of the summit, and a water cistern on the north side. Take in the well-earned views: look north to Hozomeen Mountain, west to Ross Lake and the Picket Range, south to Jack Mountain and its impressive Nohokomeen Glacier filling its cirque, and east to Skagit Peak. You can also see Snowfield, Eldorado, and many more peaks. To the east, look down to Lightning Creek, running north and south, with Three Fools and Freezeout creeks running eastward from Lightning.

Return the way you came.

9 NORTH MOUNTAIN

YEAR CONSTRUCTED	LOOKOUT ACCESS	LOCATION
1966	Catwalk open to public; undergoing restoration to permit overnight rentals (estimated completion in 2019)	Mount Baker–Snoqualmie National Forest, Darrington Ranger District

Roundtrip distance: 2.4 miles
Elevation gain: 570 feet
Lookout elevation: 3824 feet
Map: Green Trails Darrington No. 78
GPS coordinates: N 48° 18' 33" W 121° 23' 21"
Permits and fees: None

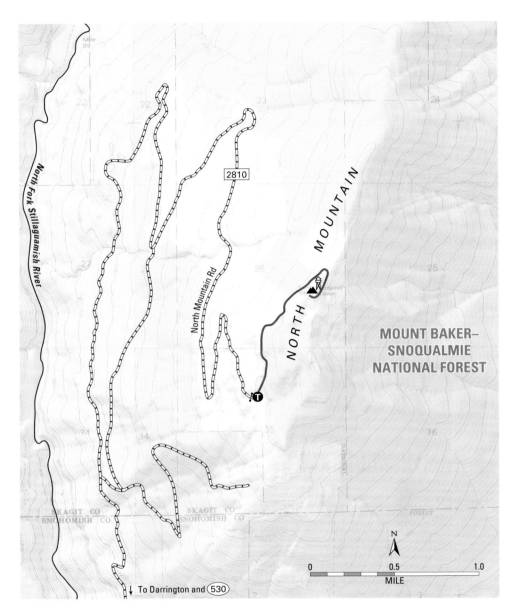

GETTING TO THE TRAILHEAD

From the intersection of Mountain Loop Highway and State Route 530 Northeast in Darrington, follow SR 530 (Emens Avenue North) northward for 1 mile (passing the Darrington Ranger Station on your left at 0.6 mile). Turn left onto Forest Road

2810 (North Mountain Road), signed for Whitehorse Park. Follow the main forest road, ignoring any spur roads. The pavement turns to gravel at 2.9 miles, and you'll reach the gate at 12 miles. Park before you reach the gate without blocking it. There are several spots to pull over and camp on the way.

> Just outside the town of Darrington, you don't have to drive far or hike long to get stunning views of river valleys, Puget Sound, forested foothills, and big, glaciated peaks.

ON THE TRAIL

This is a pleasant, shady walk on the final stretch of road before the summit. Walk around the gate on the gravel road and up through hemlock, alder, and Douglas fir trees. At around 0.7 mile, the forest opens up briefly, and you may be able to catch a little sunshine and some peekaboo views of Mount Baker to the northwest (your left) and get a taste of what's to come. You may also see huckleberries and a few maples, as the gentle but steady grade takes you higher.

North Mountain Lookout and Mount Baker

Catwalk at North Mountain Lookout with view east to Glacier Peak Wilderness

At 1.15 miles you'll see a sign for the outhouse to your right, and immediately after that, round the corner, and the lookout comes into view. You will reach the base of the tower at 1.2 miles and 3824 feet. From the base of the lookout, ascend the 53 steps to the wraparound catwalk.

This is a very late construction in Washington fire-lookout history. While many other lookout towers were being torn down in the 1960s, North Mountain was just starting as a fire-lookout site. In 1962, the US Forest Service began sending staff up to North Mountain with a tent and firefinder. Then in 1966, the permanent structure that you see today was built—a fourteen-by-fourteen-foot R-6 cab on a forty-foot tower. Characterized by a flat roof with overhanging eaves, this is one of three existing R-6 flat cab lookouts in the Mount Baker–Snoqualmie National Forest, along with Lookout Mountain and Heybrook. It remained in active service through the 1980s, but was abandoned in the '90s and unfortunately saw a lot of vandalism after that.

But its history has taken a turn for the better. This lookout is an active example of citizens taking pride in local heritage and stepping up to preserve the structure so that it can be enjoyed by the public for years to come. In 2013, the Friends of North Mountain formed, with the aim of restoring the lookout so that it could be used as a rental. Volunteers completed a tremendous amount of work, including reframing the structure, completing a historic inventory, and receiving a determination of eligibility for the National Register of Historic Places. All the restoration is being done according to the Secretary of the Interior's Standards for the Treatment of Historic Properties. The organization ran a Kickstarter campaign in 2016 to raise money. If you want to get involved, they are always accepting donations that go straight to covering the cost of repairs, and they host regular work parties, too. Check out www.northmountainlookout.com for more details. By 2019, the lookout should be completely restored and open to the public for overnight rentals in the summer months.

You can take in the varied, 360-degree views from the catwalk. To the east, look down to the Sauk River with the long ridge of Prairie Mountain behind that, and glaciated peaks beyond, starting with the tip of Glacier Peak poking up, then White Chuck Mountain to the south, followed by the pointy knobs of Mount Pugh and Sloan Peak. To the northeast are the North Cascades and the tight cluster of the jagged Picket Range. Mount Baker is due north, plus Mount Shuksan to the east of that. Due south is Whitehorse Mountain and to the southwest, look down the North Fork Stillaguamish River valley all the way out to Puget Sound and the Olympic Mountains.

Return the way you came.

10 GREEN MOUNTAIN

YEAR CONSTRUCTED	LOOKOUT ACCESS	LOCATION
1933	Closed to public, except when staffed by volunteers occasional summer weekends	Mount Baker–Snoqualmie National Forest, Darrington Ranger District

Roundtrip distance: 8.4 miles
Elevation gain: 3300 feet
Lookout elevation: 6500 feet
Map: Green Trails Cascade Pass No. 80
GPS coordinates: N 48° 16' 05" W 121° 45' 47"
Permits and fees: Northwest Forest Pass to park

GETTING TO THE TRAILHEAD

This trailhead entails quite a long drive on forest roads; plan accordingly. From Darrington, go north on State Route 530 northeast for 7.5 miles, turning right

Looking up to Green Mountain Lookout from the trail

immediately after the Sauk River bridge onto Forest Road 26 (Suiattle River Road). After 10 miles on FR 26, the pavement changes to gravel. At mile 11 you'll enter the Mount Baker–Snoqualmie National Forest, and at mile 15 you'll pass Buck Creek Campground. After 19 miles, veer left onto FR 2680, signed for Green Mountain Trail. Reach the trailhead at 21 miles, with parking on the right (south) side and the trailhead on the left (north). There is a small sign that says "Green Mountain Trail," but there is no parking lot. Park on the south side of the road. There are several designated campgrounds along the forest road on the way in.

> Well suited to either a day hike or overnight, scenic Green Mountain is just north of the Suiattle River. It is named for the huge, green meadows visible for miles, but if you go in fall, it becomes a "red" mountain with spectacular fall colors.

ON THE TRAIL

The trail starts on the north side of the road. Walk about 100 feet before you reach the trail register and sign for Trail #782. It's mercifully shaded on a hot day, and the trail is well maintained. At about 1.25 miles the views will start to open up, and you'll see the surrounding peaks.

The trail is thick with vegetation. Brush past tall thimbleberry bushes, vine maples, ferns, and moss hanging from trees as you climb steadily. At 1.75 miles you enter Glacier Peak Wilderness, and to the southeast Glacier Peak is indeed visible. At 2.7 miles the trail drops gently down into sloping meadows.

In another hundred feet or so, you are in an unofficial camping area at around 5250 feet, with tarns to the left and right of the trail. The tarns are shallow but clear, and make a decent water source if you camp here or need water en route. There are about five to seven campsites, and no permit is required to stay overnight, but make an effort to camp only in established spots. There is an ancient privy in very poor condition.

From here, the lookout is visible up ahead in the distance. These green meadows give the mountain its name, but if you come in the fall, the sloping hillsides are orange and a fiery, almost-purple red. Enjoy the vibrant colors from a large, flattish meadow at 3 miles and 5450 feet before the trail starts climbing steeply again. Just beyond 3.5 miles, you will start to see views to the north. Finally, with a last little push upward, you reach the 6500-foot lookout in 4.2 miles.

There are plenty of good spots to sit, have a snack, and enjoy the views of the Suiattle River valley, Glacier Peak, Fortress Mountain, and Buck Mountain to the south. Southwest is White Chuck Mountain, and due east is Dome Peak. Mount Baker, Mount Shuksan, and the Pickets rise to the north.

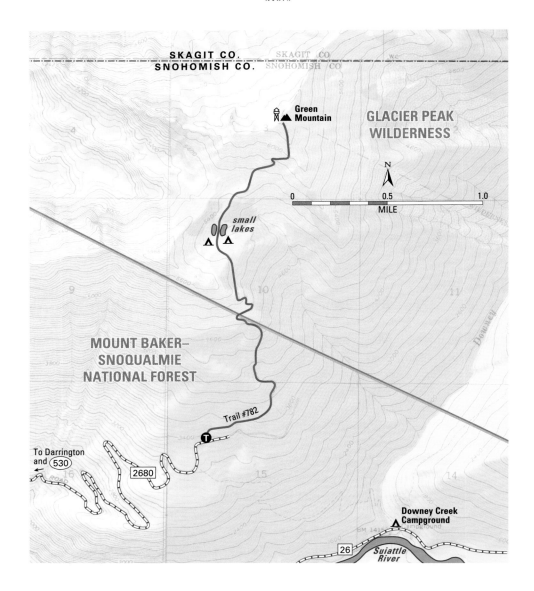

Green Mountain has been used as a lookout site since 1919, and the structure you see today was built in 1933 by the CCC. It served a brief stint in the Aircraft Warning Service during World War II, and remained in active service as a fire lookout until the 1980s. It fell into disuse, and parts began to rot, leading the building to be condemned in 1995. Efforts were made to restore the structure, but that led to more issues: a wilderness preservation group based in Missoula, Montana, filed a lawsuit

Green Mountain Lookout

against the federal government in 2010 on the grounds that using machinery and helicopters in repairing the lookout violated the federal Wilderness Act.

Local citizens and organizations advocated for keeping the lookout, but in 2012 a US District Court judge in Seattle ruled that the US Forest Service needed to remove the structure. In 2013, two of Washington State's representatives introduced the Green Mountain Lookout Heritage Protection Act in the US Congress. The act was to amend the Washington State Wilderness Act of 1984 to specifically allow for the operation and maintenance of the lookout. Washington State's US senators backed the bill, arguing that its passage would support tourism in the Darrington area, especially needed after the devastating effects of the March 2014 mudslide in neighboring Oso. The act was signed into law by President Obama in April 2014 to the relief and celebration of local residents who cherish the lookout for its history and gorgeous views.

Green Mountain certainly had a rough go of it the last couple decades, between the lawsuit, the condition of the structure, and the closure of the Suiattle River Road from 2003 to 2014. The colorful history adds to the value of this site today, as new life is breathed into the lookout. In 2016, Washington Trails Association (WTA) conducted a pilot program, in partnership with the US Forest Service, to staff the lookout with volunteers during designated summer weekends. Not expected to do any actual fire spotting, the volunteers interacted with hikers, helped maintain safety, and fostered leave-no-trace etiquette. The lookout will undergo more restoration, and the status of future volunteer programs has not yet been determined. Contact the ranger station for the most up-to-date information. Return the way you came.

11 MINERS RIDGE

YEAR CONSTRUCTED	LOOKOUT ACCESS	LOCATION
1953	Staffed; locked when not staffed (catwalk may or may not be open)	Mount Baker–Snoqualmie National Forest, Darrington Ranger District

Roundtrip distance: 30.6 miles
Elevation gain: 4610 feet
Lookout elevation: 6208 feet
Map: Green Trails Glacier Peak No. 112
GPS coordinates: N 48° 14' 40" W 121° 48' 34"
Permits and fees: Northwest Forest Pass to park

GETTING TO THE TRAILHEAD

This trailhead entails quite a long drive on forest roads; plan accordingly. From Darrington, take State Route 530 northeast. Just after crossing the bridge over the Sauk River at 7.5 miles, turn right (east) onto the Suiattle River Road. Follow the road for 22.7 miles until it ends at the Suiattle River Trailhead; at 10 miles the pavement ends and you continue on gravel. Note the separate parking for livestock and for hikers. Privy available. There are walk-in campsites at the trailhead and campgrounds on the road in.

> This multiday backpack to one of the most remote lookouts in the state wanders along the verdant Suiattle River and then climbs steeply up a ridge in the heart of Glacier Peak Wilderness, with abundant water and camping options along the way.

ON THE TRAIL

Settlers have accessed Miners Ridge for copper mining claims via the Suiattle River since 1900. A road that extended back to the current trailhead was completed in

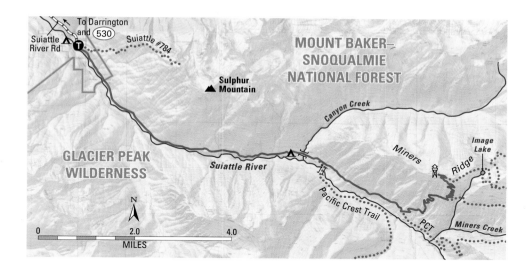

1968, and it saw a lot of flood damage between the 1970s and early 2000s, including fourteen floods that caused enough damage to qualify for federal aid. The Suiattle River Road was closed for major repairs in 2003 and 2006, reopening in October 2014, all fixed and dramatically changing accessibility into Glacier Peak Wilderness.

The trail starts at the end of the Suiattle River Road, on the east side of the parking area, signed Suiattle #784. You'll reach the trail register in another 400 feet. Starting just under 1600 feet, you will stay at a fairly level elevation along the Suiattle River for the next 7 miles, with only minor undulations taking you closer and farther from the riverside, while gradually gaining some elevation (around 900 feet). Enjoy this flattish beginning through the lush, primordial river valley.

You'll start by seeing big evergreens like Douglas fir, western hemlock, and western red cedar, including a handful of beautiful old-growth specimens, along with thick, bushy trailside vegetation of maple, alder, goatsbeard, salal, and abundant fern varieties. And if the timing is right, don't miss the chance to graze on the assortment of berries right next to the trail: thimbleberry, huckleberry, native trailing blackberry, and salmonberry.

Not only do you get some flat miles and plenty of snacks, but there are nearly endless options for campsites—and consequently, many choices for breaking up your mileage. Reach the first option at 2.9 miles, a campground on the right (south) of the trail, right on the river. At 4 miles, just past a creek, reach another campground and bench. At 5.6 miles, another campground, this time on the left. One of the biggest camping areas is at Canyon Creek at 6.6 miles and 2400 feet. There is a large bridge, with multiple sites before and after the river, and easy water access. All camping is on a first-come, first-served basis.

At 6.9 miles and 2530 feet, you will reach a trail junction. This is the rerouted Pacific Crest National Scenic Trail (PCT), which was extended a few miles west from its original route when the huge Suiattle River bridge was completed in 2011 (after a catastrophic 2003 flood washed out a smaller bridge upstream). Note that this section of trail will not be on maps printed before 2011. Going right would take you to the river; however, stay left on the PCT northbound to start a tiny bit of climbing. Even though the trail gets steeper, there are still a handful of flat spots and established campsites.

You will cross another couple of streams, and it's a good idea to fill up here if needed, as the terrain is only going to get drier. As you leave the river valley and gain some elevation, it's fun to watch the vegetation change and witness the astounding biodiversity on this trail. The forest is bursting with flowers, like bluebells, yarrow, rock penstemon, Solomon's seal, bunchberry, and ocean spray. Keep your eye out for the funkier little growths, like Indian pipe and pink wintergreen.

Reach another junction at 9.4 miles. Straight would keep you on the PCT, but go left, signed for Image Lake. On a hot summer day, this is quite a climb, going up 3320 feet from here in the next 5.5 miles. Tighten your backpack straps, eat a snack, sip water, and get ready to push. It's tough, but let the variety of plants take your mind off your burning quads. You may see pearly everlasting, white rhododendron, spotted coralroot, and pipsissewa. Your next benchmark is another junction at 12.7 miles. There is a campsite here, and staying straight (east) would cut you over to Suiattle Pass. But (surprise!) you're going uphill, to the north (your left).

As you get even higher, relish the pretty subalpine meadows as you start to see lupine, pink and white mountain heather, Cascade blueberries, and subalpine daisies, along with subalpine fir and white pine dotting the slopes. Finally, you will reach the ridge at 14.9 miles and 6100 feet. Take this moment to catch your breath and take in the incredible surroundings at this trail junction. To the south, towering Glacier Peak nearly smacks you in the face. You can now see over the north side of the ridge that you have been climbing and look into the Canyon Creek valley and toward Dome Peak.

You're going left (west), but to the right (east) is an indisputably worthy side trip if you have the time (more on that later). For the lookout, go left for the final short ridge walk. You can see the tower lookout ahead and just have to cross a pretty flower-filled meadow and go up the last 100 vertical feet and a little more than a third of a mile to

OPPOSITE *Western anemone and Miners Ridge Lookout*

Hiker on Miners Ridge, Glacier Peak Wilderness

get there. When you reach the lookout at 15.3 miles, slip off your pack, and let it soak in how far you are from . . . anything.

From this remote, lofty perch, you will feel absolutely embraced by wilderness. Gaze on the Ptarmigan, Vista, Ermine, and Dusty glaciers of Glacier Peak, while the winding Dusty Creek and Vista Creek flow into the Suiattle River far below. Looking down, you'll hardly believe how far you just came up. Enjoy the wall of peaks to the southeast: Fortress, Chiwawa, and Dumbbell mountains and Helmet Butte.

This lookout is still staffed by volunteers. Interested in volunteering here? It's possible! Contact the ranger station for more information. Some volunteers sign up for multiple years, so there are not always openings, but sometimes new staff are needed. Apparently, it's not an uncommon lookout to staff as a couple—at least half a dozen newlywed couples have spent a honeymoon summer there. The season I visited, it was a married couple who had both retired from the National Park Service. They alternated days off, so that one could hike out, run errands, and resupply while the other continued to watch for fires. Lookout staff will usually have supplies brought in by pack animals, but if the trail conditions are unsuitable for livestock, staff may need to haul everything in themselves.

The lookout you see today is the third structure on this site. The first was a shake cabin from the mid-1920s. In 1938, a twenty-foot tower cabin similar to today's was built. Finally, in 1953, the L-4 tower structure with catwalk you see was constructed. In the 1930s, there was an average of three visitors per year to the lookout; now there are thousands. Inside, the original equipment is still in use, like the Osborne Firefinder with its map from 1962 and the traditional safety stool with glass feet. If staff do need to call in a fire, they use a radio repeater powered by a four-battery bank charged by solar panels.

Return the way you came, unless you want to take a side trip to Image Lake, which you do. No, really; if you've come this far, you cannot miss the quintessential views from this backcountry gem. Walk the 0.4 mile back to the ridge junction, and continue straight along the ridge for about 0.7 mile. If you want to camp, stick to established sites at least a quarter mile from the lake. At the lake you'll find a must-see reflection of Glacier Peak in the subalpine lake waters. It's such a beautiful site, and a prime example of the need for conservation and the improvements that can happen with a little effort. In the 1960s, the lake was in bad shape, and the area around the shore was denuded due to heavy use. With the regulations now in force, the lake is cleaner, and vegetation has returned. Livestock are prohibited at the lakeside and must be kept in a separate camp away from the lake; fires are prohibited within a quarter mile of the lake. Also, note that in summer the flow in and out of the lake is very low, and swimming is discouraged.

From here, return to the ridge junction, and from there, return to the trailhead the way you came.

12 MOUNT PILCHUCK

YEAR CONSTRUCTED	LOOKOUT ACCESS	LOCATION
1938	Open to public for day use; overnighting on a first-come, first-served basis	Mount Baker–Snoqualmie National Forest, Darrington Ranger District

Roundtrip distance: 5.4 miles
Elevation gain: 2200 feet
Lookout elevation: 5324 feet
Map: Green Trails Granite Falls No. 109
GPS coordinates: N 48° 04' 12" W 121° 11' 06"
Permits and fees: Northwest Forest Pass required to park; Verlot Public Service Center

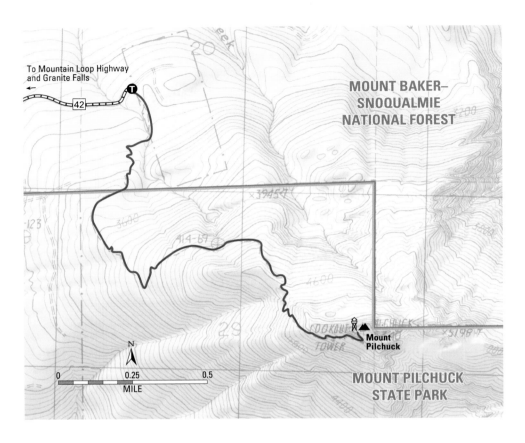

GETTING TO THE TRAILHEAD

From Granite Falls, go north on the Mountain Loop Highway and proceed 10 miles to the Verlot Public Service Center. Continue 1 mile past the public service center, cross a bridge, then take the next right onto paved Mount Pilchuck Road. Once you've made the right turn, look for a sign indicating the road is Forest Road 42. Proceed 6.8 miles down this road, and you will reach the parking lot, which is just off the trailhead (with restroom) for Mount Pilchuck. The last mile is unpaved and contains potholes, so drive with caution. Break-ins are common at this trailhead; as with parking at any trailhead, do not leave valuables in your car.

Its proximity to Seattle and relatively short trail contribute to this hike's popularity. Brave the crowds to see stellar 360-degree views, the open lookout, and its wealth of historical interpretive information.

ON THE TRAIL

You will start on a shady trail of hemlock and fir and gain elevation gradually. There is a lot of moving water in this first section, and the trail can be pretty damp in places, even in late summer. At 1.1 miles you will reach a lichen-dotted boulder field with views that include Mount Rainier and hamlets to the south. This is the first place you'll see the plastic-wand trail markers—and you'll see them many more times. The trail is rocky and often transitions from being a traditional dirt path as you frequently cross big boulders. Enjoy a brief, flatter patch and start to get views to the left of Puget Sound and Mount Baker to the north.

At 1.5 miles, as the trail becomes stone steps, keep your eye out for the safest, marked way to follow the trail. At 1.8 miles, just as you feel like you're getting farther removed from civilization, you encounter a huge concrete slab on your right. What? It was the anchor for the lookout's hand pulley, used to cable items up and down the mountain. As you look up at the elevation still to gain from here, it seems like an ingenious setup.

As you go up, enjoy the uncommon sight of the hillside rocks, an almost Sierra-like blotchy-granite cliffside. Around 2.4 miles the trail will dip slightly, and when it slopes upward again, you'll have to pass through a narrow opening between two vertical slabs of granite. Be patient here on busy days, as it creates a bit of a bottleneck since only one hiker can pass at a time. Continue up and up, hitting a wooded section again, until you reach the saddle at 2.6 miles. You can look across to the east side of this ridge for the first time. And you're almost there!

Hikers on the Mount Pilchuck summit with views west to Puget Sound

Rock scramble on last section to Mount Pilchuck Lookout

Veer left (north) to follow the trail a little farther before it disappears into a pile of boulders. This last little section is a scramble. It's suitable for children and beginning hikers, but take your time to pick out the way toward the lookout that feels safest. There are big gaps between rocks, and a fall could be dangerous. Half of the challenge of this section is that it gets very crowded, adding to the hectic feel and the imperative to be patient and intentional in your movement.

Finally, you reach the base of the lookout and climb the short, vertical ladder to get onto the catwalk. After 2.7 miles and 2200 vertical feet of effort, you are now on an incredible perch of narrow summit with views in all directions. Take in the dizzying ring of Western Washington topography: To the southeast are Mount Stuart, Gunn Peak, Baring Mountain, and Mount Index. To the west in the foreground are the cities of Granite Falls, Everett, and Marysville, followed by Whidbey and Camano islands in Puget Sound. Across the water, you see peaks of the Olympic Peninsula, including Mount Constance, the third-highest peak in the Olympics. To the north are the Twin Sisters peaks, Mount Baker, and Mount Shuksan.

To the northeast are Whitehorse Mountain, the Three Fingers, and Eldorado Peak. Squint and see if you can make out the dot of a lookout on Three Fingers South

Peak—and wonder how the heck people get up there (read more in Hike 13). To the east are White Chuck Mountain, Mount Pugh, Glacier Peak, Mount Dickerman, and Sloan, Bonanza, Vesper, and Gothic peaks (many of the primo hikes off the Mountain Loop Highway).

After you gawk from the catwalk, check out the interpretive and historical info inside the unlocked lookout. Signs inform you that a trail up Mount Pilchuck was built in 1909, and that this site had been in use as a lookout from as early as 1918—when it was just a tent and a firefinder, as was common before cabins were constructed. In preparation for a structure to be built, the US Forest Service began installing phone lines, built a tramline to haul supplies up starting in 1920, and in 1921 blasted off a portion of the summit to create a flat spot. They then constructed a D-5 twelve-foot-by-twelve-foot cabin with a cupola.

The present fourteen-by-fourteen-foot L-4 ground house was built in 1938, remodeled in 1942, and last staffed in the 1960s. As part of the Washington State centennial in 1989, the Washington State Parks and Recreation Commission partnered with the Everett Branch of The Mountaineers to restore and maintain the lookout. The partnership raised money from local citizens and businesses, and volunteers spent innumerable hours making the lookout as historically accurate as possible. It was listed on the National Historic Lookout Register in 1993.

Return the way you came.

13 THREE FINGERS

YEAR CONSTRUCTED	LOOKOUT ACCESS	LOCATION
1931	Open to public for day use; overnighting on a first-come, first-served basis	Mount Baker–Snoqualmie National Forest

Roundtrip distance: 15 miles (plus additional 19 miles roundtrip by foot or bicycle between parking and trailhead)
Elevation gain: 4200 feet
Lookout elevation: 6850 feet
Maps: Green Trails Granite Falls No. 109 and Silverton No. 110
GPS coordinates: N 48° 11' 37" W 121° 13' 42"
Permits and fees: Northwest Forest Pass to park; Verlot Public Service Center

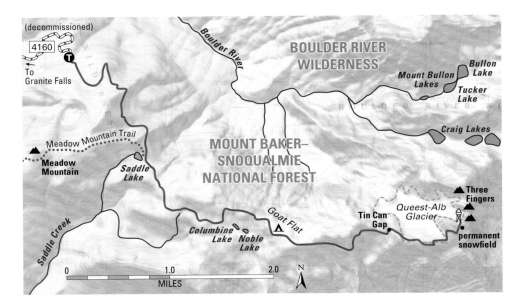

GETTING TO THE TRAILHEAD

From Granite Falls, go north on the Mountain Loop Highway. Follow it until Milepost 7 at the top of a hill, where you will see two telephone poles set close together on the left. Turn left here, onto Forest Road 41. Stay on the main road until the pavement ends at 1.8 miles. Continue straight up the hill and follow this road until it ends at 8.6 miles. You will reach an impassable bridge blocked by large boulders, and this is the unofficial trailhead. The official trailhead is another 9.5 miles ahead on the overgrown forest road. There are several pull-over spots on the drive in on FR 41 where you could camp, as well as campsites on Canyon Creek at the end of the road (an unofficial trailhead). The great irony: this is one of the closest lookouts to the Seattle area, but also the hardest to access. It is the only technical route covered in this book, and requires mountaineering skills and comfort with exposed scrambling. But to say it's worth the effort is a massive understatement.

> *Three Fingers—it is doubtful that man has ever erected a house atop a more formidable foundation.*
> —*Ray Kresek,* Fire Lookouts of the Northwest

ON THE TRAIL

Did I mention that Three Fingers is special? Not only is it a technical hike (ice axe and crampons recommended), but the challenges start before you even get to the trailhead. Due to an unsafe bridge across Canyon Creek, the forest road is closed to motor vehicles for 9.5 miles before the trailhead, which most people choose to mountain bike to. If you can get your hands on a bike trailer, I would recommend it; riding uphill for nearly 10 miles with a backpack will be some serious work for your quads. The trailhead is marked with a fallen-down sign around 3000 feet, and you'll likely see bikes stashed nearby, locked to trees.

Right away the trail is unforgiving and it feels like you're walking up a gouged, narrow streambed. It's rocky, rooted, and has some big steps up. It is in dense forest until 1.75 miles, when the trail opens up and makes a welcome shift into packed dirt. At 3800 feet and 2.4 miles, you reach the Meadow Mountain Trail junction. Stay to the left (south) toward Goat Flat, and you'll immediately see Saddle Lake to the right of the trail.

At 3.25 miles and 4250 feet, you reach a small meadow with a stream. If you did not top off your water supply at Saddle Lake, this is a good spot to do it. The trail continues its steady climb for another mile and a quarter, until you reach the subalpine splendor of Goat Flat at 4.6 miles and a reassuring "Welcome to Goat Flat" sign. Look down to heather and wildflowers and up to soaring views of Mount Rainier, Puget Sound, the Olympics, and the three dramatic peaks ahead. This established

Three Fingers Peaks with the lookout precariously perched on southernmost (right) peak

Three ladders on the final portion of the ascent to Three Fingers Lookout

camping area has a handful of unofficial sites and a privy. A permit is not required for overnight camping, as these aren't designated sites, but do try to camp in an already established site to minimize impact. There are murky tarns, and there may be nearby streams running earlier in the season, but if you are planning to camp, it's recommended that you carry the water you need from one of the two previously mentioned water sources.

Continue past Goat Flat, and at 5.5 miles you will see scree fields wrapping around the south slope of the ridge where the trail switchbacks upward to reach Tin Can Gap. You have almost 500 vertical feet to ascend in half a mile, and it's a shadeless, south-facing section, so be sure to protect yourself from the sun.

Arrive at the small but momentous saddle of Tin Can Gap at 6 miles and 5800 feet. This is a good place to catch your breath, hydrate, snack—and gawk at the vista in front of you. The Queest-Alb Glacier is visible directly below. What used to be one large glacier is more like a collection of small ones, due to recession and snowmelt, but it's still a huge mass. You can see the Three Fingers in the distance: North Peak to the far left, Middle Peak, and the tallest, South Peak, on the right. You can barely make out the white speck of the fire lookout on the South Peak, and most people at this point might wonder how the heck they are going to get all the way up there. It's okay to turn around here; getting to Tin Can Gap is a gorgeous and worthy hike, especially if you can overnight at Goat Flat.

For those who want to continue to the lookout, hold on to your hats—things are about to get serious! You can see the long ridgeline directly south of the glacier. The trail dances between the top, the south side, and the north side of this ridge for the next 2 miles. If there is still snow, technical skills may be necessary—ice axe and possibly a rope and crampons. Check trip reports and wait until it has melted out later in the summer. Even when it's snow-free, take care in windy conditions, as the trail is narrow and fairly exposed in places.

You follow the trail up onto the ridge before dropping down around the south side. It's a skinny but well-defined path, with a steep slope dropping downward. Then the trail again passes over the top of the ridge and skirts down the north side. It gets pretty steep right here in a small gully, and luckily a fixed polyethylene rope serves as a handline. Depending on your comfort level (and how long your legs are), you could hike this little section unaided by the rope, either facing forward or downclimbing. I found the rope helpful. At the bottom of that section, the trail skirts about 5 feet from the glacier. In heavy snow years or early in the season, you may walk on steep snow briefly before the trail bops back over to the south side of the ridge, around 7 miles and 6100 feet.

The final section is the diciest. With about 0.75 mile to go and 750 feet of elevation to gain, the trail ends, and you reach the bottom of a small permanent snowfield. When there is a lot of snow, the easiest route would be straight up the snowfield with crampons and an ice axe. However, in a low-snowfall year or when much snow has melted out at the end of the season, it's possible to continue ascending on the rocks around the left (northwest) perimeter of the snowfield. This option requires some rock scrambling, likely following cairns.

Three Fingers Lookout

Above the snowfield, there is a tiny bit more scrambling up and to the left (north). This takes you to the north side of a tiny ridge, and the Queest-Alb Glacier is again visible—thousands of feet below as you peer from a small ledge. Stay focused on crossing the ledge to reach the ladders. Three wooden, vertical ladders are affixed to the rock right below the lookout. Take care with a large pack, as one of the ladder transitions between rocks is a bit narrow. Finally, finally, the last little bit: at the top of the third ladder is another handline to assist you on the steep, smooth rock face before you get to the "front porch" of the lookout. Take a moment to let your heart slow down as you realize what an absolutely incredible and improbable perch you have just reached.

Once that sets in, your next thoughts might be, "Why did they decide to put a lookout here, and how on earth did they get supplies up?" Three Fingers was first summited in 1929 by a Darrington district ranger and another local climber to determine if it would be possible to put a lookout there. Their optimistic conclusion: it would take work but was not impossible. In 1930 the trail was cut and the telephone line hung; in 1932 the building was guyed into place; by 1933 it was ready for a resident.

One of the first lookout residents was Harland Eastwood in 1936. This is a great line from Ira Spring and Byron Fish's book, *Lookouts*, talking about Eastwood: "Even without a right arm, lost in an accident, he was a remarkably deft woodsman."

You can imagine that kind of man would marry a hardy, unconventional lady, and indeed it seems so: he brought his new wife to Three Fingers that summer for their honeymoon.

In order to make room for the lookout, the top fifteen feet of the granite spire had to be blasted away with dynamite, and even so, the lookout barely fits on the summit. It takes up about half of all the walkable surface area. The room is comfortable, with a double bed platform, a chair, low counters for cooking on, and a firefinder in the middle. The lookout has a well-visited and homey feel with games, decks of cards, historic photos, leftover dry foods, and other odds and ends.

This is a wonderful lookout to visit as either a day hike or an overnight. During the day, you can take in the stunning views of what feels like half of Washington State. From the North Cascades and Mount Baker over to the east to Glacier Peak, down south to Mount Rainier and west to Puget Sound, Seattle, and the Olympics, this is an all-encompassing vantage point. It's a dramatic place too, as the east side of the peak drops straight down about 2400 feet, and the headwaters of Spire Creek is a half mile away and 4000 vertical feet below.

For most lookouts available on a first-come, first-served basis, later arriving parties understand that they won't be staying in an already occupied lookout, but Three Fingers is not one of those. Based on how difficult it is to get to, and that the only campsites are way back at Goat Flat, it's understood that multiple parties may end up overnighting together. There is space for six people to sleep relatively comfortably (two on the bed and four on the floor). I recommend lowering the shutters before bed, as it can get incredibly windy, and the shutters will likely bang throughout the night. Another thing to note: there are no facilities up here. If you stay the night, bring a human waste disposal kit.

The lookout was only in active use for about a decade, and was then abandoned until the 1980s. The Everett Branch of The Mountaineers formed the Lookout and Trail Maintenance Committee in 1985, and those good folks have been caring for the lookout ever since. In 2015, they undertook a massive reroofing project that involved airlifting materials and more than 400 hours of volunteer-only labor.

Return the way you came, using extreme caution descending the first 0.75 mile on the ladders, rocks, and snowfield.

14 MONUMENT 83

YEAR CONSTRUCTED	LOOKOUT ACCESS		LOCATION
Cupola cabin, 1930; tower, 1953	Catwalk open; lookout closed to the public		Access through E. C. Manning Provincial Park, BC; lookout in Okanogan National Forest, Pasayten Wilderness, Methow Valley Ranger District

Roundtrip distance: 19 miles

Elevation gain: 2840 feet

Lookout elevation: 6520 feet

Maps: Map Town Manning Park 092H02; ITMB Manning Park/Skagit 92H2/3

GPS coordinates: N 49° 03' 24" W 120° 44' 21"

Permits and fees: None to park, enter park, or day hike; $5 per person, per night to camp

GETTING TO THE TRAILHEAD

Note: *Trailhead is in Canada; visitors are responsible for the proper documentation to cross the border.* From the Manning Park Visitor Centre at E. C. Manning Provincial

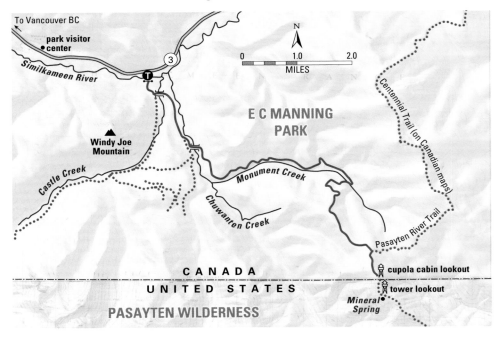

Original cupola log cabin, on Canadian side, and current Monument 83 Lookout tower on US side

Park in British Columbia, drive east on BC Highway 3 for 1.5 miles. Turn right where it's signed for the Monument 78/Monument 83 trails. You have reached the trailhead, where there are two large lots with privy available. Designated car camping and wilderness camping is available throughout the provincial park. This trail is a semipopular winter recreation spot for cross-country skiing and snowshoeing, though the lookout isn't necessarily as popular, as it's a lengthy day trip.

Also called Holdover Peak Lookout, this one is best approached through Canada, where the shortest route is still almost 10 miles each way. You get the distinction of visiting the northernmost lookout in Washington—inches from the international border. It is possible to reach the lookout from the US side, but it's a 60-mile trek, usually done as a loop through the Pasayten Wilderness.

ON THE TRAIL

I'll tell it like it is: this is not the most scenic hike, as you head endlessly through partially dead forest and keep moving to avoid the biting flies. But what the journey lacks, the destination makes up for with views, two structures, and most likely, complete solitude. Even the ranger at the visitor center looked at me quizzically and, polite but incredulous, said, "What do you want to go to Monument 83 for?"

Start at the gate on the south side of the parking lot, and begin walking on a wide, flat trail. The forest is lined with thimbleberry, aster, wild rose, fir trees, hemlock, and Solomon's seal. At 0.4 mile, cross a wood and metal bridge, and then 100 feet later, you'll reach a junction and stay right for Monument 83. You are walking on a mountain bike double-track road edged with horsetail and thistle. At 0.5 mile, you'll cross a small wooden footbridge.

By 0.6 mile, you'll start to see one of the major downsides of this trail: the effects of the pine beetle evident in the blackened pine needles. These pests have devastated forests across northern Washington and British Columbia, including more than 40 million of the 136 million acres of forest in BC. It may be the largest forest-insect blight ever seen in North America. Mountain pine beetles affect pine trees by laying eggs beneath the bark and by introducing blue stain fungus into the sapwood that prevents trees from repelling or killing the attacking beetles with tree pitch flow. The fungus also blocks water and nutrient transport within the trees, resulting in popcorn-shaped blobs of resin on the trees' exteriors. The joint action of larval feeding and fungal colonization basically girdles trees, killing them within a few weeks.

Because these trees are dead, they are more likely to get blown over in a windstorm. Always use extreme caution in areas of pine beetle blight; keep moving, listen for creaking, and never, ever camp under dead trees.

The trail is pretty gentle so far. You go up just over 100 feet in the first mile. At 1.2 miles, go left (east) at the signed junction. The forest is a mix of live and dead trees, with ground cover of lupine, clover, wild strawberries, and yarrow. You reach another bridge at 2.2 miles, and then you encounter some uphill sections. You'll reach over 4100 feet before the trail mellows out again, and then alternates between flat and gentle uphill sections. By 4 miles you'll have passed several small creeks, and unfortunately, probably a lot of biting flies. Long pants and sleeves are recommended, as well as a game plan for eating. Walk and snack? Drape a jacket over you? Expect them to be relentless—if they're not, you can be pleasantly surprised.

Cross Monument Creek at 5.25 miles, and again at 6 miles. This is the last reliable source of water, so fill up here if you need to. Now the ascent becomes more consistent and moderate but still shaded. By 7 miles, you're at 5500 feet. You reach the ridge at 7.8 miles and 5951 feet. You'll also hit a very dead section, and remember to keep moving; this is not the place to stop and rest. Reach the junction with the Pasayten River Trail (also called the Centennial Trail on Canadian maps) to your left at 8.7 miles, but you want to stay straight on the main trail.

LEFT *Hiker on catwalk at Monument 83 Lookout* **RIGHT** *US-Canada border marker designating the eighty-third survey marker on the forty-ninth parallel, with the lookout just inches from the border*

By 9.25 miles you reach a meadow and the tree density opens up. Shortly, you can see the structures up ahead. First, you'll arrive at a cupola cabin, which was the original lookout structure built in 1930. Continue on and you'll pass the grave of Pasayten Pete, a rocky gravesite with a wooden headstone. The inscription says, "PASAYTEN PETE — SHOT BY L.E. LAEL — 26.8.21." There is a poem about Pasayten Pete inside the cabin, and many people have mused upon the mystery of who the heck Pete was. Now we know that he was a pack mule who had to be shot when he broke his leg in 1961. Keep going about 50 more feet to reach the base of the modern tower lookout at 9.5 miles. It's a large and grassy summit area. The peak itself is called Holdover Peak, but the lookout is named Monument 83 due to the border marker.

This has been a fire-watch site since the 1920s, when there was only a crow's nest platform to watch from. Why two structures? The twelve-foot log cabin with sheet-metal cupola that you see today was built in 1930 and became the northernmost fire lookout in the United States. As you can see though, it's set back from the edge of the rounded hilltop and does not have the best view. It's open to the public, and the inside has a table, stool, shelves, and a little ladder up to the cupola. You can stay there, but probably don't want the company of the rodent remnants and the grime that the broom can't sweep away.

The US Forest Service built the other structure, an L-4 cab on a thirty-foot tower, in 1953 for better visibility. Then the US-Canada border was resurveyed in the 1960s, and it was determined that the cabin was now on the Canadian side, making it the southernmost lookout in BC and assigning the status as northernmost lookout in the United States to the newer tower structure. This lookout was in active use until 1987.

The tower is right next to the silver Monument 83 border marker, which is the eighty-third surveying marker on the forty-ninth parallel. Looking east and west from here, you can also see the swath cut in the forest to delineate a physical border. Climb up the tower and watch your step. One step is completely missing, and there are many raised nails that need to be pounded in. The lookout is shuttered and cabled, but the shutters hang about three-quarters of the way down, so the door is not completely covered in case you want to peek in.

Whether or not the lookout is open, you have access to the wraparound catwalk, with views to the southeast, south, and southwest—which makes sense since that's the US side. The Pacific Crest National Scenic Trail (PCT) crosses the border nearby—it's about 7 miles west as the crow flies.

Standing on the deck, you can't help but wonder how lookout staff got all the way up here, 30 miles from the closest trailhead on the US side. In the 1940s and '50s, it was common for the staffer to make the trek with a trail crew working in the Pasayten for the summer. The staffer would be alone at the lookout until the crew swung back by at the end of summer, and they would all hike out together. But it was a haul; by the 1970s, staffers were brought in to the lookout via helicopter from the Methow Valley.

If you stay on the summit and are in need of water, Mineral Spring is about two-thirds of a mile down the trail south on the US side. The trail is faint and difficult to follow. Just as the trail disintegrates under some large fallen logs and gets swampy, you've made it! Listen for the trickling of water, and you should be able to find the source of the spring.

Return the way you came.

15 SLATE PEAK

YEAR CONSTRUCTED	LOOKOUT ACCESS	LOCATION
1956	Closed to public; no access to deck	Okanogan National Forest, Methow Valley Ranger District

Roundtrip distance: 0.7 mile
Elevation gain: 280 feet
Lookout elevation: 7440 feet
Map: Green Trails Washington Pass No. 50
GPS coordinates: N 48° 44' 16" W 120° 19' 16"
Permits and fees: None

GETTING TO THE TRAILHEAD

From the intersection of State Route 20 and Lost River Road in Mazama, follow Lost River Road, turning left (northwest) at the intersection with Goat Creek Road. Pass the Mazama Store, on the right on this continuation of Lost River Road. The pavement ends at 6.7 miles. You'll enter the Okanogan National Forest at 7.2 miles, where there are some dispersed- and designated-camping areas and the road becomes Forest Road 5400. At 9 miles, the road curves to the right and is signed for Harts Pass. This road is known for being "the most dangerous road in Washington," but the only nerve-wracking part comes around 12 miles, where the road narrows, curves, and has a drop-off without a guardrail or shoulder. Otherwise, the road surface is in good condition, and the road is a typical forest road. You reach Harts Pass at 19 miles, where there is a designated-camping area and pit toilet. From the Harts Pass parking area, stay to the right (signed for Slate Peak) and continue until you reach a closed gate at 21.3 miles.

This is an itsy-bitsy hike with a big driving endeavor—on the highest and most white-knuckling road in Washington, until the road ends and you cannot believe you got your car somewhere so remote. This is also the second-highest-elevation lookout in Washington.

ON THE TRAIL

Although it is less than a mile roundtrip, this hike feels like epic hiking by osmosis. This is where you take non-hiking visitors to impress them with our incredible state

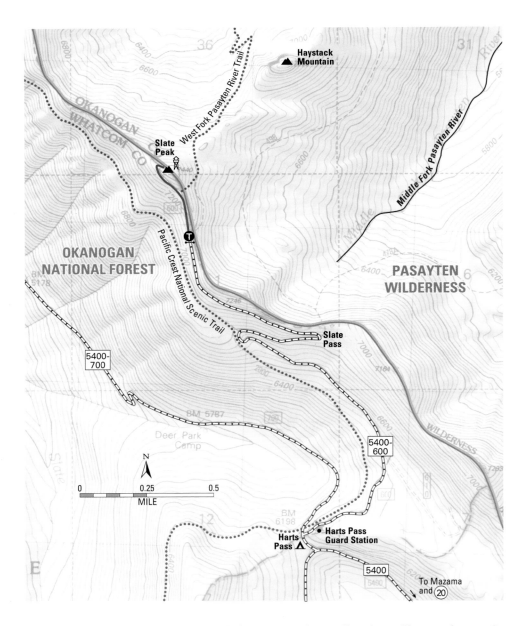

with minimal physical effort expended. To get to the trailhead, you'll cross the Pacific Crest National Scenic Trail (PCT)—the last spot that intersects with a road before the final northern stretch of trail to the Canadian border. If you visit at the right time of late summer or early fall, you may meet PCT thru-hikers looking for a lift to or from the Mazama Store for their final resupply. Don't forget that before you venture onto a road this high you should always check that it is open, as conditions change quickly, and snow may linger into late summer.

What the heck is a road doing all the way up here, anyway? It was constructed as part of a Cold War–era defense project. Slate Peak had been a fire-lookout site since the 1920s, a tied-down structure with a narrow, rocky trail leading to it. During World War II, it was used as a lookout site as part of the Aircraft Warning Service. The original cupola lookout was replaced with an L-4 cabin in the early 1950s, before the military decided to blast the summit area and build the road a few years later. They removed forty vertical feet from the top to create a wider area to install radar. Unfortunately, by the time the project was completed, the radar was obsolete and no longer needed, and a ground house lookout could not effectively spot fires, since the view would be obscured by the wider edges surrounding the structure. In 1956, the current lookout was built on a forty-foot tower to restore the original height for the view.

From the parking area, walk past the gate and continue up the road. You'll gain almost 300 feet on this short jaunt, so be prepared for a steady uphill climb. At around 0.2 mile you'll intersect the West Fork Pasayten River Trail on the north side

Silhouette of Slate Peak Lookout

North Cascades sunset from Slate Peak

of the road, reminding you that you are walking along a prime gateway to the vast wilderness of the North Cascades. Continue hoofing it up the hill until you reach the tower lookout at a gravelly summit area at about one-third of a mile.

The stairs are chained closed at the bottom with an "Unsafe to Climb" sign. From the base you can take in the tall tower in addition to a shed, storage building, and solar panels.

As you can imagine, a lookout at this high an elevation is prone to being struck by lightning; it once caught on fire after being hit. "The bolt melted a keg of nails into one solid mass," according to Ira Spring and Byron Fish in *Lookouts*.

This is an excellent place to work on your peak identification skills with the aid of the interpretive plaques around the summit outlining the surrounding peaks, many of them rising more than 8000 feet: To the west are Snowfield and Colonial peaks, Mount Baker, Jack Mountain, the Picket Range, Tamarack Peak, and the Pasayten River valley. To the south, you'll spy Gardner Mountain, Silver Star Mountain, The Needles, Tower Mountain, Golden Horn, Azurite Peak, and Mount Ballard. Devils Peak is due east, with the Pistol Peaks beyond that. To the north, gaze upon Pasayten and Osceola peaks, Mount Lago, Lake Mountain, Shull Mountain, and Three Fools Peak.

Miners began flooding this area in the 1880s in their search for gold. They traveled for days to get to this remote area, and set up camp on the hillside. In the 1890s they were supplied by the store and tavern in the new town of Barron. By the early 1900s, it had become a ghost town as the veins of gold disappeared. But small mines came and went for the next forty years, leaving remnants of tunnels, machinery, and shafts.

Return the way you came.

16 GOAT PEAK

YEAR CONSTRUCTED	LOOKOUT ACCESS		LOCATION
1950	Closed to public; deck accessible on lower level; staffed as needed		Okanogan National Forest, Methow Valley Ranger District

Roundtrip distance: 3.5 miles
Elevation gain: 1400 feet
Lookout elevation: 7001 feet
Map: Green Trails Mazama No. 51
GPS coordinates: N 48° 39' 4" W 120° 35' 53"
Permits and fees: Northwest Forest Pass required at trailhead

GETTING TO THE TRAILHEAD

From its intersection with Lost River Road in Mazama, drive east on Goat Creek Road for 1.9 miles to its junction with Forest Road 52. Turn left and follow it 2.7 miles until the junction with FR 5225. Turn left onto FR 5225 and continue for 6.2 miles until the junction with FR 200, and a sign for "Goat LO." Turn right and then

Goat Peak Lookout

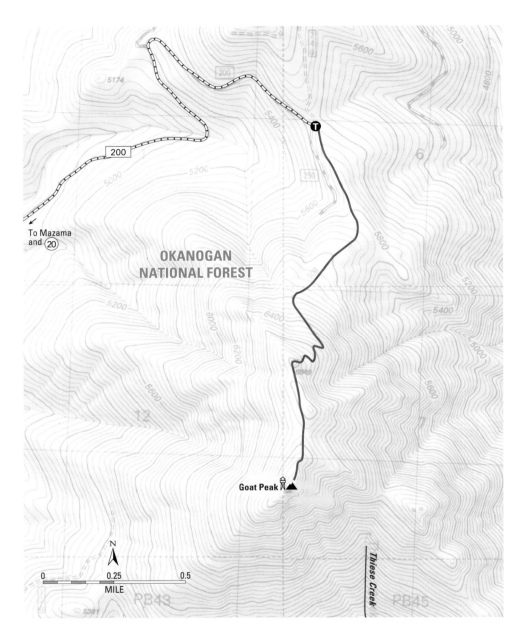

continue 3 miles to the trailhead. There is no signboard specifically for the Goat Peak Lookout Trail, but the road ends in a parking lot. There is a privy and one sign at the south side of the lot that says "Trail."

This short and dramatic hike on the eastern slope of the North Cascades visits one of the last recently staffed lookouts in the Methow Valley and a prime larch-viewing area in the fall.

ON THE TRAIL

The trail wastes no time ascending. You'll pass through firs, grassy tufts, and dappled shade with immediate views to the west. After 0.25 mile, the trail flattens slightly and moves into full sun. By 0.3 mile though, you're back in the shade as the trail climbs again, with views opening up to the left.

Here is where the trail really gets steep. You have about 1000 feet to gain in the next 0.8 mile. By 0.6 mile from the trailhead, the larches on the slope ahead come into view, and you can see the top of the ridgeline that you are aiming for. With the incline and the loose, rocky trail surface, this is a good hike for trekking poles, especially on the way down. Even though the trail is short overall, this section is challenging and exposed, so make sure to bring plenty of water and sun protection.

The big upward push ends at 6830 feet and 1.2 miles. You reach the north end of the ridgeline, and the lookout is just a half mile ahead to the south, on the far end of the ridge. This is the kind of hiking I love—up high, flat trail, and views all around. Silver Star Mountain comes into view to the southwest. Enjoy the larches, the visual layers of the dry, lower peaks in the foreground, and the jagged, tall granite and glaciers farther away.

You'll reach the summit and the lookout at 1.75 miles and 7001 feet and take in the 360-degree views. The first lookout here was a cupola built in 1923, and the site was used as an Aircraft Warning Service station during World War II. The lookout you see today is an L-4 cab from 1950 perched on a fifteen-foot tower.

Goat Peak is a prime example of what I call a "sister lookout"—it has several other lookouts in sight that could be used to triangulate on a fire. From here you can see Slate Peak, Mount Leecher, Lookout Mountain (Methow Valley), and North Twentymile Peak, all with lookout structures still standing.

My favorite part about this structure? The cocktail deck on the first floor, under the second story deck, the only one like it I've ever seen. Well, it might not technically be called a cocktail deck, but if I were living here, that's what I would use it for. It's the type of spot that makes you want to curl up with a blanket, a book, and a thermos of tea (or hot toddy) and just enjoy the view for hours at a time. This vantage point is unique, because it's farther west than most lookout sites in the Methow—right where big peaks meet the valley—so you get a more intimate look at the mountains than you do from Lookout Mountain or Mount Leecher, for example. Observe the quilted pattern of roads, burns, hills, clearings, forests, glaciers, and sharp peaks.

Hiker taking in the view from Goat Peak

Due north is McLeod Mountain. You can peer northwest toward Harts Pass (before Slate Peak) and the expanse of the Pasayten Wilderness. Prominent peaks to the south include Silver Star and North Gardner mountains. The only volcano visible is a sliver of Glacier Peak to the southwest. To the southeast, gaze down the long expanse of the Methow Valley.

Before being stationed at his current spot on Mount Leecher, Lightning Bill staffed this lookout for twenty years. He estimates that when he first started at Goat Peak in the late 1980s, there were approximately 200 to 300 visitors per year. Now there are around 2500 per season. (Learn more about Bill in Hike 19.)

When you've had your fill of the view, return the way you came.

17 NORTH TWENTYMILE

YEARS CONSTRUCTED	LOOKOUT ACCESS		LOCATION
1923 and 1947	Tower lookout closed; deck is open to public; cupola ground house may be open to public		Okanogan National Forest, Methow Valley Ranger District

Roundtrip distance: 12.6 miles
Elevation gain: 4390 feet
Lookout elevation: 7437 feet
Map: Green Trails Coleman Peak No. 20
GPS coordinates: N 48° 42' 09" W 120° 53' 42"
Permits and fees: None

GETTING TO THE TRAILHEAD

From the intersection of the North Cascades Highway (State Route 20) and West Chewuch Road in Winthrop turn left onto West Chewuch Road, which is signed for Methow Valley Ranger Station. In 6.75 miles reach the junction with the Eastside Chewuch Road (which comes from Winthrop) and continue north, now on Forest Road 51. Follow this paved road for another 11.2 miles, turning right onto FR 5010 just beyond the Camp Four Campground. Cross the Chewuch River and bear right at the Y intersection, heading south on FR 5010. After 0.5 mile bear left onto FR Spur 700, and follow this somewhat rough road 1.6 miles to the trailhead and small parking area just before a gate.

> The third-highest lookout in Washington State! And as a nearly 13-mile-roundtrip hike with not one, but two lookouts at the top, including the only standing cupola lookout in the Cascades, this hike really packs a punch. Be prepared to pass through a lot of burned forest to get there.

ON THE TRAIL

While it may sound obvious, it bears reminding: hiking on the east side of the Cascades is pretty different from the west side, and hiking through a burn is its own beast, too. As soon as the trail starts, you may notice how sandy it is—the result of forest fire and the soil composition changing because so much organic matter got incinerated. Be prepared for the feeling of walking in ashy sand and the smudge marks to show for it.

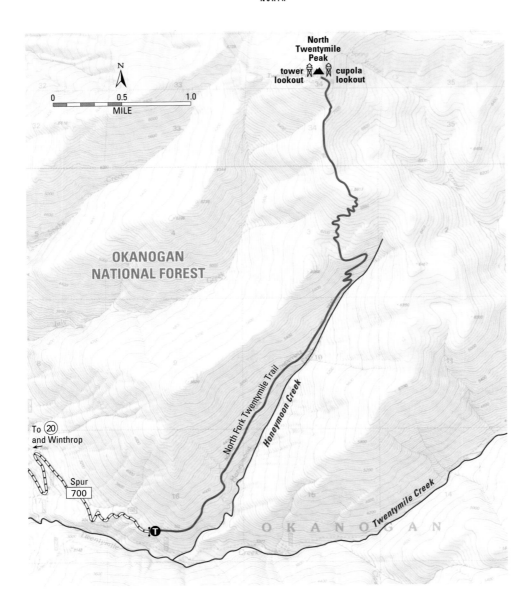

As the trail slopes gently upward, another big difference you'll notice is the smell. It might be the California lilac (Ceanothus), midsize native bushes whose leaves emit a sweet fragrance. You are in the very welcome shade of larger trees, and it's likely already really warm, even first thing in the morning.

By half a mile in, the trail starts ascending moderately, and the trees become less dense. You can hear Honeymoon Creek rushing in the valley far below to the east as you come into full sun in an area with tufts of grass instead of trees. Then the trail takes a sharp left (west) away from the creek and you will be back to trees. By 1.25 miles you start to encounter more logs and debris on the trail, and the bushes are really overgrown. I highly recommend wearing gaiters on this hike—it might be too hot for pants, but your legs will get scratched up if they are not covered. The trail is not difficult to follow, but you do have to keep a close eye on it through the dense brush. It feels like barely anyone has walked this trail in years.

You will start to get into the heart of the burn remnants from the 2006 Tripod Complex Fires, and by 2 miles in, you can see burned trees on the slope across the river valley as well. Tall fireweed sprouts all around in what I call the telltale chromatics of a burn: the dead-tree white, the charcoal-black burned stumps, the vibrant green of undergrowth, and the bright pink of the fireweed. It is supremely quiet in this recovering forest: just the occasional grasshopper and languid buzz of a big fly. At 3.25 miles the switchbacks begin, and more life appears in the forest—chipmunks, bugs, and songbirds.

At 4 miles you reach a full-on burn and the subsequent fireweed jungle. In another half mile or so, the views will start to open up at around 6600 feet. Now it feels like we're getting somewhere! The trail flattens out at 4.9 miles, and then you catch your first glimpse of the tall 1947 tower lookout. Enjoy a flattish 1 mile before climbing again. This is your last push, and the lookout feels close, standing sentinel on the ridge above an expanse of dry yellow grass.

North Twentymile tower lookout and original cupola

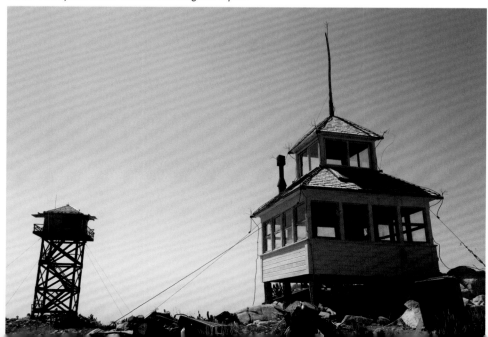

You reach the summit at 6.3 miles and 7437 feet. That's high! As you might expect, it's windy up here, and layers are recommended even on a hot day. The newer lookout is a fourteen-by-fourteen-foot structure on a thirty-foot tower—constructed long after this design was in vogue. Just climbing the 38 steps and pushing open the unlocked, but heavy, trapdoor in the howling wind can feel like a feat, not to mention walking on the catwalk. The lookout itself is locked, and has not been officially staffed since 1987. If the shutters are open, you can see a bed, sleeping bag, jugs of water, stove, desk, chairs, bench, counters, and most impressively, the original firefinder in the middle of the room.

The other lookout is the historic twelve-foot-by-twelve-foot cupola ground house from 1923—so historic in fact, that it is the only one you will see in the Cascades. (Monument 83 has one as well, but technically it's in Canada.) It was renovated in 2016 and may be open to the public when you visit.

The view, if there is not any wildfire smoke, will be nothing short of magnificent. It feels like you're in the dead center of the Okanogan National Forest. Peer west, into the heart of the Pasayten Wilderness, at Big Craggy Peak, Mount Lago, and McLeod Mountain. North you're looking at peaks toward the Canadian border. You can see Silver Star Mountain to the southwest. East you're peering toward Loomis Mountain. Tiffany Mountain is southeast. To the south is the Sawtooth range, which separates the Methow Valley from Lake Chelan.

Return the way you came.

18 LOOKOUT MOUNTAIN (METHOW VALLEY)

YEAR CONSTRUCTED	LOOKOUT ACCESS	LOCATION
1937	Closed to public; catwalk accessible	Okanogan National Forest, Methow Valley Ranger District

Roundtrip distance: 3.2 miles
Elevation gain: 1150 feet
Lookout elevation: 5515 feet
Map: Green Trails Twisp No. 84
GPS coordinates: N 48° 19' 27" W 120° 48' 55"
Permits and fees: None

OPPOSITE *Fireweed after a forest fire*

GETTING TO THE TRAILHEAD

From State Route 20 in Twisp, turn southwest onto Second Avenue, following signs for the Twisp River Road. Take the first veer to the left at 0.1 mile onto Lookout Mountain Road. At 2.2 miles you'll see a sign for Forest Road 4345-200. Follow this road for 6.5 miles to a wide, flat parking area (no privy or signboards).

Get into the heart of the Okanogan Highlands and enjoy the expanse of dry, grassy hills and big, granite peaks.

ON THE TRAIL

Start in the flat, decent-size parking area. You could drive a tiny bit farther up the road, but it gets steep quickly, and there are only a couple parking spots. Instead, walk the first 250 feet up the steep section after which the road gradually narrows into an overgrown track, then finally, a trail. Stroll on the moss-lined path through the Douglas firs and ponderosa pines. Watch your step as you keep ascending—there are some loose, golf ball–size rocks on the trail.

The view to the east starts to open up just before 0.3 mile, where the trail turns west as you pass through a fence. Enter a small grassy meadow on a slope with views to the north, before the trail switches back to head east again.

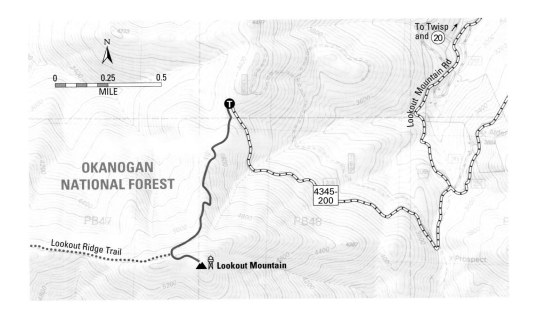

Reflection of Methow Valley in windows of Lookout Mountain Lookout

Around 4950 feet and 1 mile, you'll reach a small, flatter section with views to the west. Catch your breath briefly before the climb starts again, now on the western flank of the slope. The sides of the trail start to feel a little more rocky and subalpine—like you are getting close to the top of something.

You will wrap around toward the east and start to crest the ridge. At 1.2 miles you will get your first views south as you reach a junction at 5350 feet. To your right is the Lookout Ridge Trail, which leads to a campsite, and then beyond to the west. Stay left as the trail reaches the ridge and the view to the south opens up to the expanse of the Sawtooth Ridge. The lookout comes into view up ahead at 1.3 miles. Enjoy this last bit of ridge walk, a gorgeous amble flanked by golden grasses, scrubby bitterbrush, and gnarled, stunted trees.

You'll reach the lookout at 1.6 miles and 5515 feet. This L-4 cab looks like it's seen better days. It's unpainted (or rather, the paint is all peeled off) and has a Wild West feel, between the scrappiness of the building and the dry, sage-dotted landscape. There are no signs stating that ascending is prohibited, but the partially ripped-off lookout door doesn't help the haphazard feel. Use extreme caution if you go up, and enjoy the expansive views. Sister lookout Mount Leecher is 10 miles southeast as

Lookout Mountain Lookout

the crow flies. To the east you can see various drainages such as Libby Creek, Benson Creek, and Canyon Creek, with the Columbia Plateau beyond. To the north and northeast are intimate views of the Methow Valley, and the more distant northern peaks of Old Baldy, Tiffany Mountain, and North Twentymile.

Looking west offers great variety as rolling brown knolls reach the tree-covered hills, rising back into bigger rocky peaks. See the jagged outcroppings of the North Cascades featuring the likes of Gardner, Patterson, and Robinson mountains, and Goat Peak.

This site has been used as a camp lookout since the second decade of the twentieth century. A log cupola cabin was built in 1931, and the current L-4 cab on a twenty-five-foot tower was built in 1937. Similar to Goat Peak and Slate Peak lookouts in this area, Lookout Mountain was used as part of the Aircraft Warning Service in the wintertime during World War II. Lookout staff would pack in supplies on snowshoes, 2.5 miles at the time. The building was staffed regularly during the summer until the late 1990s. It's a strategic spot, and lookout staff made many first reports of fires each season. As the US Forest Service has employed fewer lookout staff in the Methow, Lookout Mountain has been staffed only periodically—the last time was by Lightning Bill for a full season in 2005, and for just a month in early summer in 2008, when there was still too much snow on Goat Peak. (Learn more about Bill in Hike 19.) The structure is on the National Historic Lookout Register.

Return the way you came.

19 MOUNT LEECHER

YEAR CONSTRUCTED	LOOKOUT ACCESS	LOCATION
Crow's nest, around 1920; tower, 1939	Staffed in summer; accessible to public when invited in by staff; locked when not staffed	Okanogan National Forest, Methow Valley Ranger District

Roundtrip distance: 2.5 miles
Elevation gain: 520 feet
Lookout elevation: 5008 feet
Maps: Partial on Green Trails Twisp No. 84 and Loup Loup No. 85; USGS Knowlton Knob with summit on Twisp East
GPS coordinates: N 48° 14' 15" W 119° 0' 33"
Permits and fees: None

GETTING TO THE TRAILHEAD

From the visitor center in Twisp, go east on State Route 20 for 2.5 miles and then turn south onto SR 153 (Methow Valley Highway). Follow SR 153 south for 3.1 miles, and

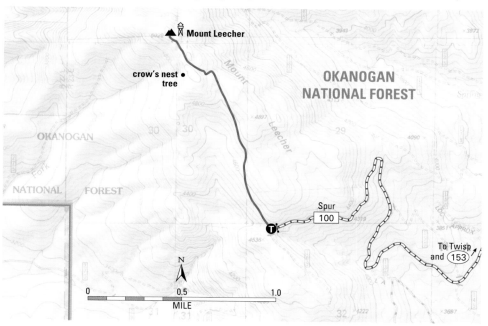

then turn left on Benson Creek Drive. The pavement ends at 2.3 miles. Follow this road for 9.9 miles to the junction with Forest Road Spur 100 (signed for Leecher LO). Turn right and follow FR Spur 100 for 3.5 miles to the gate. If the gate is unlocked, you can drive all the way to the summit at 4.7 miles. If the gate is locked, or you prefer the walk, park on the shoulder here without blocking the gate.

Visit a still-staffed lookout at a primo vantage point in the Okanogan Highlands, with a century-old crow's nest narrowly rescued from a 2014 fire.

ON THE TRAIL

Assume the gate will be closed, and if it's not, then you have an option to drive. But where is the fun in that? Park on the shoulder, being careful not to block the gate, and start your hike on the dirt road. It's a pleasant stroll through evergreen trees and, if the season is right, wildflowers. You gain elevation steadily and pass patches of burned pine, evidence of the 2014 fire. The trail offers intermittent shade on a hot day, and you will start to see more firs as you get a little higher.

At 1.1 miles the lookout tower becomes visible. Soon you'll reach the ridgeline, which the road follows northward as you start to get views to your left (west). You'll pass a storage shed before reaching the lookout in 1.25 miles.

The lookout is staffed in the summer (June or July until September or early October, depending on the fire risk), so give a friendly shout or let the staff notice you before you ascend the tower. If the staff is not there, the trapdoor to the catwalk will be locked, and the lookout inaccessible. Otherwise, you will most likely hear a shouted invitation to "Come on up!" Either way, climb the 54 stairs to the top of this forty-foot tower to get a better view. Remember that this is someone's home, and it's best to arrive during "business hours" (9:30 AM to 6:00 PM). If you are invited in, you can see the 360-degree view from the catwalk, the firefinder on its stand, and residential furnishings such as a bed and kitchen items. Notice a bucket hanging off the side of the lookout? It's full of rocks, and acts as a counterbalance in an ingenious solution to make opening the heavy wooden trapdoor more manageable.

There have been a dizzying number lookout structures on this site, starting with a crow's nest around 1920. Fire watching was done from a wooden tree platform with sleeping and cooking at a camp down below. A ground house was built in 1921 for sleeping, and in 1932, there came a unique design (and one you don't see in the Cascades anymore): a forty-foot steel watchtower with a six-by-six-foot cab on top.

OPPOSITE *Original ladder to the nearly century-old crow's nest at Mount Leecher*

Mount Leecher Lookout

According to Ira Spring and Bryon Fish in *Lookouts*, during World War II, the ground house was moved to Twisp to be used as an Aircraft Warning Service station. To replace it, the US Forest Service brought the L-4 lookout from Chiliwist Butte that had originally been built in 1939. In 1953 the steel tower was removed, and the L-4 cab was hoisted onto a new forty-one-foot tower. The lookout was closed for a bit in the 1980s, likely due to lack of funding, but is now in good shape after $65,000 in renovations to the structure in 2009.

Lightning Bill, possibly Washington's most experienced fire watcher, currently staffs the Leecher Lookout. He first began staffing lookouts in 1978 at Chelan Butte (which is no longer a lookout site, but the structure is still intact at the Columbia Breaks Fire Interpretive Center in Entiat; see Bonus Lookouts). He staffed the Goat Peak Lookout for twenty years, and then moved back and forth between Goat Peak and Mount Leecher in 2014 and 2015. As of 2016, he was assigned to staff Mount Leecher full-time, and is expected to continue this assignment through at least 2017, depending on the needs of the forest service.

The view from the top of the tower is phenomenal. Looking south you see the Columbia River, Wells Dam, and the Chelan Divide, moving toward the Sawtooth Ridge to the west. To the immediate west is the town of Carlton, with the eastern slope of the Cascades beyond. To the east, the closest ridge is Jay Ridge, then you see the Colville Reservation, continuing east toward Spokane. To the north are Finley Canyon, Loup Loup Summit, and Beaver Creek.

This spot also showcases how common it was for many lookouts to be within line of sight of each other. North of Mount Leecher are sister lookouts Goat Peak, Lookout Mountain (Methow Valley), Buck Mountain (near Loup Loup), and North Twentymile. They may be far away and hard to spot if you don't know exactly where to look—but the fact that so many are still visible is a nod to the glory days of lookouts, when there were at least thirty-five lookout structures in the Methow Valley alone.

You'll also see a lot of burned forest from the 2014 Carlton Complex Fire. The lookout staff had to be evacuated that year, but luckily the lookout structure was not damaged.

Don't miss the other highlight of the site: the crow's nest. Determine your bearing while you're still on the tower catwalk—look southeast to the ridgeline, and look for a fir tree that is very bushy at the top. That's where the crow's nest is, though the platform itself is no longer visible. To get there, return the way you came. Walk 0.15 mile down the road past the "Leecher LO" sign, and then veer right onto the ridge to the south. Follow the ridgeline for another 0.1 mile until you reach the tree with the very bushy top.

We can all be thankful that this tree was saved by a local couple in the 2014 fire. The couple called the already evacuated lookout staff and asked where the tree was, then went up there in the midst of the forest fire to dig a fire line around the tree to save it. You'll notice the tree is standing green and sentinel, while many other trees around it are burned. Though still visible, the original ladder is extremely fragile and covered with moss. Do not attempt to climb this tree or the nearly 100-year-old ladder. A nearby campsite features a stone wall, a nice flat spot, and rock fire rings. This is the original spot where staff cooked and camped at night, after spending the day up in the crow's nest watching for fires.

Return to the road and continue back the way you came.

20 BUCK MOUNTAIN

YEAR CONSTRUCTED	LOOKOUT ACCESS	LOCATION
1961	Closed; catwalk open to public	Okanogan National Forest, Methow Valley Ranger District; trail starts in Loomis State Forest

Roundtrip distance: 4 miles
Elevation gain: 1160 feet
Lookout elevation: 6135 feet
Map: Green Trails Loup Loup No. 85
GPS coordinates: N 48° 25' 30" W 119° 50' 50"
Permits and fees: None

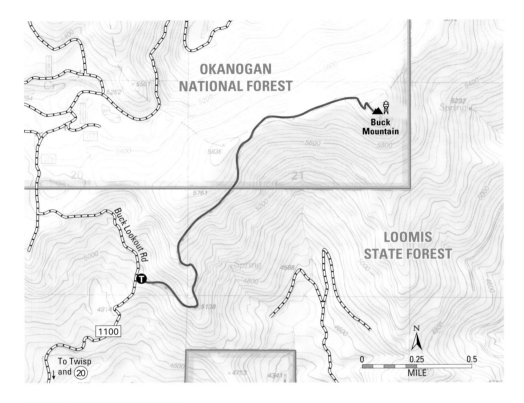

GETTING TO THE TRAILHEAD

From southeast of Twisp where State Route 20 intersects with SR 153, continue north on SR 20 for 12.8 miles (2.1 miles past Loup Loup Summit). Turn left (north) onto unmarked Forest Road 1100, also called Buck Lookout Road. Follow this road for 3.8 miles until you reach a faint spur to the right at two close-set trees. Park here, taking care to not block the road.

Camping is available off SR 20 at Loup Loup Campground, a few miles west of the turnoff for Buck Mountain.

> This short hike in a seldom-visited portion of the Okanogan passes through a quiet, beautiful landscape and an austere recent burn.

ON THE TRAIL

Begin the hike at the unofficial trailhead of two trees at around 4980 feet. Walk east on what is technically a road, but is in such rough condition with such limited pull-out or turnaround space that it's best to treat it as a trail. You will ascend steadily, and at 0.4 mile and 5140 feet you round a bend and get your first view of the lookout to the northeast! Your eye can follow the ridgeline from left to right up to the summit of Buck Mountain, with the tower lookout visible against the horizon. You may see lupine, yarrow, and wildflowers along the road and in the pretty, sloping subalpine meadows.

You will also see a massive amount of burned areas. What starts as a few charred pine trees opens up into full hillsides of decimation from the 2014 Carlton Complex Fire. The soil becomes sandier and more ash-laden as you reach the ridgeline at 0.6 mile, with bigger views opening up to the south and west. Continue upward, hitting 5600 feet at 1 mile. You get a reprieve in a slightly flat section at 1.25 miles as you gape at the surreal, stark forest now more densely enclosing you on the ridge. At 1.4 miles you will begin a more serious ascent and start catching views to the north over the ridge.

The forest is now completely bare trunks—ghostly white bark with scars of black. All vegetation like grass, shrubs, and flowers disappeared completely, but will grow back more and more every year, and you may even see new green buds sprouting. At 1.6 miles the trail goes up more steeply, and at 1.85 miles and 5970 feet, you have one last big push to the top. There is a flat section toward the summit that could be

Buck Mountain Lookout

Damage to Buck Mountain Lookout from a 2014 fire

parking for intrepid motorists, with room for about five vehicles. You reach the lookout at 2 miles and 6135 feet.

The front steps were burned during the 2014 fire, but amazingly, the rest of the lookout is intact and pretty special for that reason—a historic structure standing in the midst of a completely burned forest. You can't help but wonder how it's still standing. (Most likely it was wrapped in fire-resistant material or sprayed with foam fire retardant.) You can ascend the stairs to the catwalk, but the lookout is likely to be locked and secured with a cable. You'll see signs of use, such as a solar panel and fire pit.

This spot has been a lookout site for a long time. In 1919, the staff lived in a log cabin and spotted fires from a crow's nest in a tree. Then in 1934, an L-4 cab was constructed atop a twenty-foot tower, serving a dual purpose in 1942 as a military Aircraft Warning Service post as well as a fire lookout. From the flat roof on the current lookout, you would likely surmise that it was constructed later. Sure enough, the fourteen-foot-by-fourteen-foot lookout with catwalk that you see today was built in 1961. It is no longer staffed.

Return the way you came.

21 FUNK MOUNTAIN

YEAR CONSTRUCTED	LOOKOUT ACCESS		LOCATION
Crow's nest, 1914; tower, 1943	Unlocked but unsafe for public access		Okanogan National Forest, Tonasket Ranger District

Roundtrip distance: 0.4 mile
Elevation gain: 160 feet
Lookout elevation: 5121 feet
Map: USGS Conconully East
GPS coordinates: N 48° 35' 52" W 119° 15' 33"
Permits and fees: None

GETTING TO THE TRAILHEAD

From the intersection of North Main Street and Broadway Street in Conconully, head north along North Main Street. Once you get out of town, North Main turns into Forest Road 38. In 3.5 miles, turn right onto FR 3810 (after the Oriole Campground turnoff). Follow it for 2.1 miles, then bear right onto FR 3810-200. From here, you'll

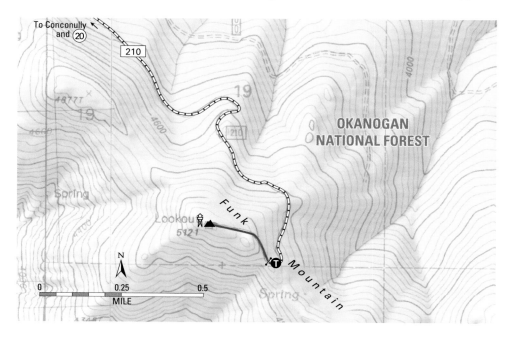

Cement pilings from original ground house at Funk Mountain

see a spur in 0.8 mile to the left; stay straight to continue onto FR 210 (with a short steep section) and drive an additional 1.7 miles to a flattish saddle on the east side of Funk Mountain. Park off the road, without blocking the gate up ahead.

There is designated camping available at Cottonwood Campground and Oriole Campground, which you pass at 2.2 miles and 2.8 miles respectively, north of Conconully off FR 38.

> This very short stroll in the far-eastern Okanogan heads to an all-but-forgotten lookout with an incredibly special feature—a 100-year-old tree platform, still intact.

ON THE TRAIL

This is the shortest hike you can do to a lookout, but it's worth it. You get to explore a corner of the Cascades that many people don't make it to, and see one of the oldest designs of fire-lookout structures remaining (a tree platform) in all the US Forest Service. Start by walking due west from the flat parking area toward a gate, which may or may not be open. Initially there is no tree cover, but there may be wildflowers such as lupine and yarrow. Very shortly you'll enter a more forested section and come under the cover of trees on the pleasant dirt road.

The lookout comes into view in 0.15 mile. Continue walking until you reach the lookout at 0.2 mile and 5121 feet. It's a small summit area with a little red outhouse. In front of the lookout steps you'll see four concrete pillars with rebar—the foundation of the first building, a 1932 ground house with a cement front doorstep on the south side of the square.

Climb the 51 steps up the tower to reach the catwalk deck. Take great care up here as, unfortunately, the lookout is not in great shape. A board on the deck is missing, and the lookout door may be unlocked, though there is a "Danger Keep Out" sign. You may find that the shutters are down but not secured, and one is completely missing.

The structure is ramshackle, but the views are not. Take in the expanse of the Okanogan Valley and the North Fork Salmon Creek. Directly south is the little town of Conconully and due east is Fish Lake. The larger peaks to the west and northwest are Muckamuck Mountain, Old Baldy, and Tiffany Mountain. Most of the land seen from Funk is outside of the national forest, which may be why using and maintaining

LEFT *Funk Mountain Lookout* **RIGHT** *1914 crow's nest in Douglas fir next to Funk Mountain Lookout tower*

the Funk Mountain Lookout was less of a priority than it was for some of the other lookouts in this area.

This site was one of the very earliest used by the US Forest Service for fire watching, beginning with a tent dwelling in 1911. A crow's nest platform was constructed in 1914, and was probably still used into the 1930s, even after the first ground house was built, since it had no cupola. Today an L-4 cab stands on a forty-foot tower, built in 1943 and used as needed until 2000. It is no longer staffed or maintained. From the northwest corner of the lookout, on the catwalk, you have a good view of the original crow's nest cradled in the closest Douglas fir, about two-thirds of the way up the tree, a little below the height of the catwalk. However, there is no ladder anymore. Old photos of the crow's nest show it at the tippy-top of the tree—it's incredible to see how much the tree has grown!

As you might guess about a site that was put into use so early in the history of lookouts, staff had to employ some of the earliest designs in fire-spotting instruments. It's rumored that the original staff at this lookout had one of the first heliographs in the area—a signaling device that reflects sunlight in flashes from a movable mirror. Heliographs can be used to send messages with Morse code, and the lookout staff here ended up training other lookout staff in the region.

Return the way you came.

22 MOUNT BONAPARTE

YEAR CONSTRUCTED	LOOKOUT ACCESS	LOCATION
1961	Staffed; accessible to public when invited in by staff	Okanogan National Forest, Tonasket Ranger District

Roundtrip distance: 5.2 miles
Elevation gain: 2210 feet
Lookout elevation: 7257 feet
Maps: USGS Havillah and Mount Bonaparte
GPS coordinates: N 48° 48' 45" W 119° 52' 35"
Permits and fees: None

GETTING TO THE TRAILHEAD

From US Highway 97 in Tonasket, turn east onto Havillah Road. Reach the town of Havillah in 16 miles and turn right onto Lost Lake Road. After 0.8 mile, stay right, now

Firefinder still in use at Mount Bonaparte Lookout

on Forest Road 33 as the road turns to gravel. At 4.1 miles, you'll enter the Okanogan National Forest, and there is a faint turn to the left (almost directly across from the sign) to a camping area and pit toilet. At 4.2 miles, turn right onto FR 300, signed for Bonaparte Trail. There is a lower trailhead in 1.2 miles, but unless you want to add a couple miles to the hike, keep driving until the trailhead is on your right at 2.5 miles.

This forested hike in the far northeast corner of the Cascades visits a staffed lookout and an original 1914 log cabin. Hikers can also approach the lookout from Bonaparte Lake via the South Side Trail #308 and connecting fire roads.

ON THE TRAIL

This is a special spot. The hike itself is forested without much in the way of views, but the drive to the trailhead and the hike to the summit are unique. This hike is the farthest east of any in this book, and it's a good excuse to explore areas that may be less familiar. A sign at the trailhead informs you that this site may have been used as a lookout (with tent) as early as 1906. The first tower was constructed in 1914, and the structure you will see today is a prefabricated lookout lowered into place via helicopter in 1961.

Mount Bonaparte Lookout with 1914 ground cabin

Start on Bonaparte Trail #306, which goes steeply upward for the first 0.5 mile. Pant your way up through the dense forest of pine and fir, cluttered with many small, young trees. Then the understory starts to thin, and you'll see a lot of dead, white, woody debris on the forest floor. This is an ATV road—wider than your typical hiking trail and deeply grooved.

At 1 mile, you reach the junction with the South Side Trail #308, which is to the left and heads to Bonaparte Lake. This is an alternate trail for hiking to Mount Bonaparte. Now around 5700 feet, stay right (straightish). The trail is all in the trees, but at 1.2 miles, get your first glimpse to your right (west) of the valley below. At 1.3 miles you reach a steep bit as the trail switches directions and turns east. You'll start to see the abandoned steeper tracts of older road, but make an effort to stay on the main, newer path.

By 2 miles the vegetation starts to change a little, and heather becomes more prominent. At 2.3 miles and 6920 feet, pass the spur to the right for the Antoine Trail; stay left on the road. After another quarter mile or so, the trees open up and it's obvious you're getting higher. You'll see an official lookout sign before reaching the top at 2.6 miles and 7257 feet. It's a large summit area with rocky ground and clustered with white bark pine.

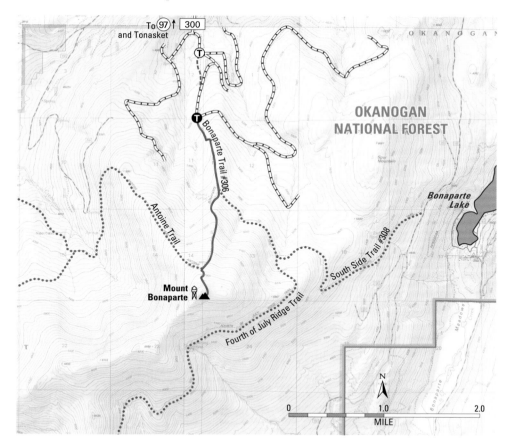

Mount Bonaparte is one of the lookout treasures that is still staffed. Remember to arrive during reasonable hours—the staff is on the clock from 9:30 AM to 6:00 PM. When I was there, the man on duty noted that it had not gotten above seventy-two degrees all summer, and the area had just gotten a dusting of snow the night before, on the second day in September. So regardless of how warm the drive in is, don't forget to bring layers and gloves as climbing a 7200-foot summit in Washington is a serious endeavor. The trail is near the Pacific Northwest National Scenic Trail (PNT), and many Bonaparte visitors are PNT hikers taking a little detour.

This is one of the few lookouts with water (for the staff) at the summit. The lookout staffer in 1929 carved a water cistern by hand out of the summit cap rock. Filled by snowmelt and rainwater, it is usually sufficient to supply the staff with water for the whole season. The cistern is still in use, and the staff treat the water before drinking it.

The Mount Bonaparte lookout is a fifteen-by-fifteen-foot R-6 flattop cab with a catwalk on a twenty-foot tower, built in the early 1960s. Before that the site hosted a tower from the 1930s. Don't miss the chance to check out the original ground cabin from 1914, which is on the National Register of Historic Places. It's made of squared, hand-hewn logs and is now used for storage. The cabin was the living quarters and had an open-air, covered lookout platform above it. Staff would watch from the platform and use a heliograph to flash Morse code to Tonasket. The platform is gone, but exercising caution and respect, you can still see the inside of the tiny cabin. Think it's just "kids these days" who crave having their existence live on in posterity and would dare to graffiti a building? Not so—you can see names scrawled on the walls in the cabin going back nearly a century! What's the oldest one you can find?

Take in views from the highest peak in the Okanogan Highlands east of the Okanogan River, and the highest for about twenty miles in any direction. Mount Bonaparte's prominence at 7257 feet makes for a fantastic lookout location. To the south is the Colville Reservation, and the dominating peaks are Mount Annie and Moses Mountain. The ridge close by is Fourth of July Ridge, and far in the distance is a wall of Cascade peaks. To the north, just a stone's throw away, is Canada, with Baldy Mountain Resort visible. The closer, brown hills are in the United States, but the green in the distance is Canada. You can also see Buckhorn Mountain and the town of Chesaw. To the east you'll see a near ridge in between the Okanogan and Colville national forests, as well as Walker Lake.

Return the way you came.

CENTRAL

23 HEYBROOK MOUNTAIN

YEAR CONSTRUCTED	LOOKOUT ACCESS	LOCATION
1964	Closed to public for day use; deck open; available for seasonal overnight rental by reservation	Mount Baker–Snoqualmie National Forest, Skykomish Ranger District

Roundtrip distance: 2.2 miles
Elevation gain: 890 feet
Lookout elevation: 1739 feet
Map: Green Trails Index No. 142
GPS coordinates: N 47° 48' 30" W 121° 32' 07"
Permits and fees: None

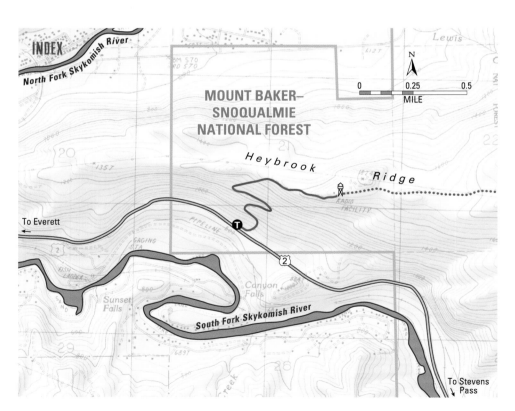

View from the deck of Heybrook Lookout

GETTING TO THE TRAILHEAD

From Everett, follow US Highway 2 east for 37.5 miles. Just past Milepost 37 and the sign for the Mount Baker–Snoqualmie National Forest, turn left into the gravel parking area on the north shoulder of the highway. Pay careful attention, as this is a winding, two-lane road with high-speed traffic, and you don't want to miss the turn or slam on your brakes. Once you are parked, keep a closer-than-usual eye on kids and pets, as cars zoom by very close to the parking area.

> This short, steep hike to one of the lowest-elevation lookouts in Washington is a great option for hiking with kids and for shoulder-season excursions.

ON THE TRAIL

While short, this hike is brilliant in its versatility. First, there is no long drive down a bumpy forest road. Heck, you could stop here on your way to or from Eastern Washington or Stevens Pass. Don't expect to move superfast as you may encounter a lot of kids, babies, and pets. It's steep enough that the short hike provides a solid challenge if you're looking for a little exercise. And as the lowest-elevation lookout in the Cascades, it gives you unique options for nearly year-round hiking.

Begin at the west end of the parking lot. Leaving the flat parking area, self-register at the trailhead kiosk, and then head out on the trail, which starts to climb immediately, the sound of the highway nearby. Soon though, the highway noise is muffled by the fir trees, cedar, and draping moss, and ferns dot the side of the trail of this young forest. Around half a mile, the dirt-and-root trail surface will present you with stairs in places.

Ascend a handful of switchbacks before the trail flattens a bit at 0.75 mile. Here the trees are less dense, the understory opens up, and light floods in. At around 1600 feet it's clear that you're higher up than where you started from. By 0.9 mile, your

Heybrook Lookout

Shady trail to Heybrook Lookout

views to the right (south) begin to expand. Not long after, you'll be able to just barely make out the lookout to the left through the trees.

You reach the lookout at 1.1 miles and 1739 feet. There is an open, gravel-covered summit area with a picnic table right below the lookout. Because the summit is surrounded by tall trees, you won't get many views from the ground; time to head up the eighty-six stairs on the sixty-seven-foot tower. This is a construction you won't see anywhere else in the lookouts in this book—there is a viewing platform underneath the lookout instead of a catwalk around it. It's essentially a large, shady deck to take in the views.

Gaze southwest to Mount Index and Bridal Veil Falls. Look southeast to Baring Mountain. Gunn Peak is due east. The South Fork Skykomish River runs northwest and southeast.

Heybrook Lookout was first built in 1925 with a platform tower, which was replaced in 1932 with an L-4 cab on a forty-five-foot tower. The structure you see today was built in 1964 of treated timber with an R-6 flat cab—one of the few R-6 designs still standing in the Cascades. The structure was abandoned in 1970, and volunteers constructed a new cab in the 1990s. The lookout was recently restored and opened for overnight rentals in September 2017. The rental season is May 1 through September 30. Reserve online through www.recreation.gov, and then coordinate deposit and rental details through the Skykomish Ranger Station.

There is no water en route or at the top; carry all that you'll need. There is an open-air toilet in the southeast corner of the summit, on the downhill slope with sufficient privacy. Walk southeast from the lookout and follow signs.

Return the way you came.

24 EVERGREEN MOUNTAIN

YEAR CONSTRUCTED	LOOKOUT ACCESS		LOCATION
1935	Closed to public for day use; open for seasonal overnight rental by reservation (see below)		Mount Baker–Snoqualmie National Forest, Skykomish Ranger District

Roundtrip distance: 2.6 miles
Elevation gain: 1370 feet
Lookout elevation: 5587 feet
Map: Green Trails Monte Cristo No. 143
GPS coordinates: N 47° 49' 35" W 121° 43' 21"
Permits and fees: Northwest Forest Pass to park at trailhead

GETTING TO THE TRAILHEAD

From Everett, drive east on US Highway 2 for 50 miles, turning left onto Forest Road 65 (Beckler River Road). Proceed on this road, which turns to gravel at 6.5 miles—stay

Evergreen Mountain Lookout

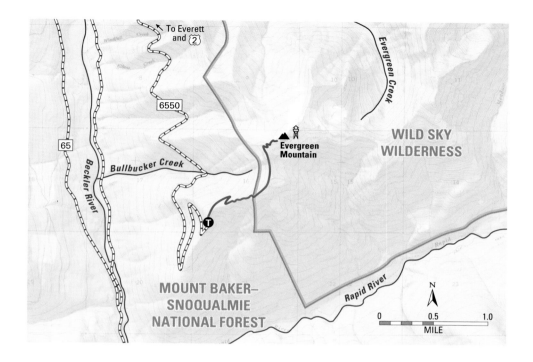

straight and cross the bridge. Continue to follow this road for 11.9 miles to a five-way intersection. Here, take the right fork (signed for FR 6550), and proceed 0.8 mile to another intersection. Turn left and drive 8.2 miles to the trailhead. Camping is available at Beckler River Campground and also at pullout spots along FR 65.

> Thanks to an online system that takes reservations well in advance, you can be guaranteed a night on the mountaintop in an original 1930s structure—or simply enjoy a gorgeous day hike near Stevens Pass.

ON THE TRAIL

Pick up the narrow trail on the east side of the road. The trail starts out verdant, shady—and wastes no time going up. Flowers like rock penstemon and lupine dot the trailside, and views of Spire Mountain and Gunn Peak to your left (west) dot the sky. At 0.25 mile, look straight down the trail to catch your first glimpse of Mount Rainier, with a sloping, green river valley in the foreground and snow-clad peaks around. Shortly after, as the trail switches back to facing northeast, catch your first glimpse of the lookout.

Any burn you see is from the 1967 Evergreen Mountain Fire burn. You're already above 4500 feet, and these slopes are bursting with subalpine flowers. You may see pearly everlasting, huckleberry, Indian paintbrush, pink subalpine spirea, and fawn lily. This flat section around 0.3 mile is open, expansive, and absolutely delightful.

At just over a third of a mile, the trail starts climbing again, and you snag some shade. By 0.5 mile, you'll enter a forest of evergreen trees, and at 0.6 mile you'll enter the Wild Sky Wilderness, the newest addition to a 2.6-million-acre wilderness area. Congress made the designation in 2008, which covers parts of the Cascade Range from Canada to Snoqualmie Pass.

You are passing through an area rich in mountain hemlock—take note of the star-bundled needle configuration. The trail hops back onto the ridgeline at 0.9 mile, revealing views to your left and right through the trees. You feel distinctly that you are on a ridge between two valleys: to your left (north), Bullbucker Creek feeds into the Beckler River, and to your right (south) is the Rapid River.

At 1 mile, you exit the forest and get a clear view of the lookout, perched above the steeply pitched green slope. Enjoy the scenic switchbacking traverse up this pretty slope—peppered with wildflowers like the white, puffy blooms of Sitka valerian and the flat, lacy tops of cow parsnip. As you get higher, the lookout gets closer, and Glacier Peak comes into view.

Reach the lookout at 1.3 miles and 5587 feet. This is the original cab, so there is no catwalk or tower, just a classic L-4 cab perched on the summit with a bit of room to walk around it. Take in the sweeping views of surrounding valleys and mountain peaks. To the south gaze upon Mounts Daniel, Hinman, and Rainier with Stuart slightly to the southeast. To the west are Merchant and Gunn peaks and Spire Mountain. Clustered to the north are Monte Cristo, Columbia Glacier, Sloan Peak, and Whitehorse Mountain, with Glacier Peak floating beyond. Nason Ridge is beyond Stevens Pass to the east. The soft meadows of Fortune Mountain and Grizzly Peak are a nice contrast to the rugged, rocky sights. You can continue another 0.1 mile down the trail to see it end—or check out the primitive vault toilet.

The fourteen-foot ground house was built in 1935 by the US Forest Service. The structure was also used year-round during World War II as an Aircraft Warning Service site. It was staffed by fire spotters during summers, who would call down to the Skykomish Ranger Station when a fire was spotted. The road in to the trailhead was (and still is) prone to washouts, making access difficult, and the US Forest Service stopped staffing the lookout in the 1980s. It was adopted and restored in the 1990s through a collaboration of several local organizations, and is now maintained by the Everett Branch of The Mountaineers and listed on the National Historic Lookout Register. It was converted into an overnight rental in the early 2000s.

A hiker and the view of Glacier Peak from the trail to Evergreen Mountain

Can you imagine calling the lookout home for a night, with the Cascades as your backyard? Reserve online (www.reserveamerica.com or www.recreation.gov) for overnight stays from late July through September. There is a two-night maximum, and the cost in 2017 was $80 per night. The reservation system usually opens in

February or March, and bookings go fast! It's like the superstar concert of the lookout world. Check the websites well in advance, but note that even when the system is open, you can only reserve dates a maximum of six months in advance. For example, on March 1, you would not be able to book a date past September 1. The lookout cabin sleeps four and is furnished with a twin-size bed and mattress, one extra twin mattress, and a table and chairs. Carry in all your own bedding, food, and water.

Return the way you came.

25 ALPINE LOOKOUT

YEAR CONSTRUCTED	LOOKOUT ACCESS	LOCATION
1975	Staffed in summer; accessible to public when invited in by staff; closed to public in off-season	Okanogan-Wenatchee National Forest, Wenatchee River Ranger District

Roundtrip distance: 9.8 miles
Elevation gain: 3000 feet
Lookout elevation: 6235 feet
Map: Green Trails Wenatchee Lake No. 145
GPS coordinates: N 47° 47' 32" W 120° 12' 19"
Permits and fees: Northwest Forest Pass to park

GETTING TO THE TRAILHEAD

From US Highway 2 at Stevens Pass, head east for 17.3 miles to the Nason Creek Rest Area. At 0.25 mile beyond (which comes very fast), turn left (north) onto the unsigned Forest Road 6910 (look for a row of mailboxes). Cross a bridge over Nason Creek, and a powerline corridor at 0.5 mile. Continue to follow the main road, avoiding side spurs. At 4.7 miles, turn right onto a narrower road and follow it for another 0.25 mile, until you reach the trailhead. A privy and a small picnic table are available. Note that much of this forest road is surrounded by private property, so it lacks the dispersed camping options that similar roads in national forests often have.

This is a special one—not far off US Highway 2, still staffed, and offering some of the best views you could hope for.

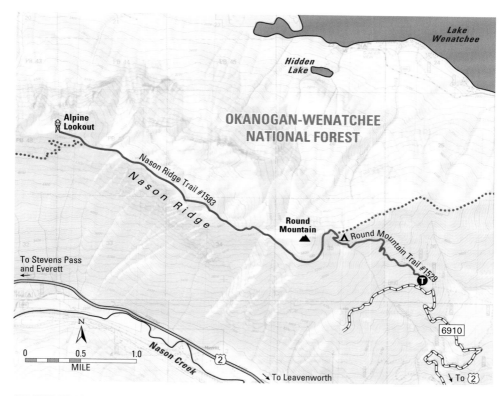

ON THE TRAIL

Pack plenty of water; you won't pass a water source, and the trail can be steep and unshaded in places. Start at the Round Mountain Trail #1529 and begin climbing immediately through a shady forest of hemlock and fir. The undergrowth is bursting with vegetation too: blueberries, bracken fern, vine maple, wild rose, and thimbleberry.

At 0.6 mile, you'll briefly pass through a burn from the concurrent 1994 wildfires at Rat Creek, Hatchery Creek, and Round Mountain. The dead, bone-white trees mean the views start to open up to the east, without the forest canopy covering you. This was part of the larger Tyee Creek Fire, a devastating burn to the east of Entiat Ridge (more details in Hikes 26 and 27). The Alpine Lookout staffer at the time was directed to stay in the lookout to monitor the area for more than twenty days in a row. He sat up there alone in the smoke-filled sky without a day off. Eventually, relief supplies and pizza were airlifted in to help boost his morale.

By 1 mile, you'll go back into a green, living forest, but you may note some conifers with dried, gnarled branches: mountain pine beetle damage. At 1.4 miles, you reach

Alpine Lookout

a junction where the Round Mountain Trail meets Nason Ridge Trail #1583—note there is also a campsite here. This could be a good place to catch your breath, as you've already ascended 1200 feet.

Go left, and in a couple minutes you'll catch views over to the north side of the mountain, looking down onto Lake Wenatchee and aloft to Glacier Peak. As you continue on a little farther, you'll start to get views to your left of a small lake and more evidence of the past burn. By 1.8 miles and around 5500 feet, the trail flattens a bit as you are now traversing the south side of Round Mountain and looking south to the Chiwaukum Mountains. Take in the subalpine fir and the sloping meadows dotted with wildflowers.

This is one of the few lookout hikes in this book that loses elevation. At 2.2 miles, you'll drop down toward the saddle between Round Mountain and Nason Ridge. At the low point, there are some flat spots where camping would be possible. By 2.5 miles, the trail starts climbing again, and it becomes clear that this is a dirt bike track. The trail is deeply grooved and recessed in places. Sometimes you'll have to choose between walking in the ditch of the groove or on the higher bank. Some parts are also rocky or rooted; watch your step.

The dirt bike section lasts until about 3 miles. At 3.3 miles, you pass through a rocky, screelike section. Go up until you reach a nice little ridge walk at 3.6 miles and nearly 6200 feet, where once again you can catch views on both sides, to the north and south, including glaciated Mount Daniel and Mount Hinman to the southwest.

Around 4.1 miles, you'll descend again slightly and get your first view of the lookout. At 4.3 miles there is a cool rocky section with a steep drop-off to your right and a view to small Hidden Lake and the Little Wenatchee River valley below. Continue on this fairly flat section, traversing the south side of the mountain that the lookout is perched on. You'll reach a signed junction at 4.5 miles, where the Nason Ridge Trail continues to the left. Stay right for the last push, continuing up the backside of this mountain. Finally, the trail switches back to the right, and the lookout comes into view straight ahead. Walk this last little stretch of summit area and arrive at 4.9 miles.

Maybe I was blown away by this hike because my expectations were low. The first time I came here, it was a rainy, misty October day with no views. When I went back on a clear, sunny day in August, I was astounded to discover the 360-degree view that had been hidden the first time. In general, I'm a fan of hiking in any weather, but with this experience it really hit home that sometimes it's worth waiting for a clear day. I have rarely seen such a sweeping view in the Central Cascades.

This site was first used for fire detection in 1920, when an outdoor alidade (the precursor to firefinders, which are alidade tables), phone, and tent were set up. The lookouts built here have always been unique or oddly timed. An L-4 ground house was constructed in 1936—past the classic L-4 era. In 1975 when most lookouts were either being restored or torn down, Alpine was completely replaced with an unusual R-6 flat-roof construction. The roof was modified to a peak roof in 2006, and the structure is listed on the National Historic Lookout Register.

Alpine Lookout is still actively used, and the staffer I met in 2016 had spent the last ten summers at this location. Wait until being invited before entering the lookout. The inside is cozy, with a bed, kitchen area, gas fridge, desk, some chairs, and a fire stand with the original firefinder. At the start of the season, supplies are still brought in on mule. Lookout staff hike out every week or two, so access to civilization is far more regular than it used to be, but a small gift of fruit or other treats is still a welcome, friendly gesture.

Back in the day, there was a railroad route through the Cascades that ran along present-day US Highway 2, and undoubtedly fires were started by embers cast off by steam engines. Fires were reported from lookouts via crank phones, and the phone line ran to a guard station in Merritt, at the foot of Round Mountain. These days, of course, they use radios, and report more than just fires. For example, there is a quarry on the north side of the mountain, and certain quarry activity can kick up clouds of dust that an average citizen will mistake for smoke and then report as a fire. The lookout staff will preemptively radio in to let the US Forest Service know that the quarry is active, and reports of smoke in that area are not in fact fire.

Whether the lookout is staffed or not, you can take in the sweeping views from the catwalk and rock foundation around the lookout. Like many lookout sites, you can see locations of former sister lookouts. Of those that are still standing, the easiest to see is Sugarloaf Lookout, visible with binoculars on a clear day. You may also spot Tyee Lookout as a small bump on the more distant ridge. The Alpine staffer reported that Tyee Lookout was easier to see when it was staffed, because the shutters would be open, and low evening sun would reflect off the windows. Now that it is no longer staffed and the shutters remain closed, it is harder to spot. There are also a handful of former lookout sites visible from Alpine where no structures remain: Poe Mountain, Mount David, and Rock Mountain. Dirtyface Mountain is also a former lookout site and now has a weather station and radio repeater that you can see.

Gazing northwest toward Glacier Peak, you can see Sloan and Bedal peaks, with Buck Mountain due north. To the east, take in the Chiwawa Ridge and the Entiat and Chelan ranges. Far south is Mount Rainier, plus Mount Stuart, Dragontail Peak, and Snowgrass Mountain. Completing the panorama, look west to the close peak of Mount Howard, and farther on Mount Hinman, Mount Daniel, and Jim Hill Mountain.

View of Glacier Peak from inside Alpine Lookout

On the north side of the lookout, look down to the two rivers. Notice a difference between them? Closer to you, the Little Wenatchee River is a dark orangey-green color, and beyond it, the serpentine White River, flowing east into Lake Wenatchee, is a milky turquoise. Even though they are close to each other, it's clear that the latter comes from a glacial source.

Return the way you came.

26 SUGARLOAF PEAK

YEAR CONSTRUCTED	LOOKOUT ACCESS	LOCATION
1949	Staffed in summer; accessible to public when invited in by staff; closed to the public in off-season	Okanogan-Wenatchee National Forest, Entiat Ranger District

Roundtrip distance: 1 mile
Elevation gain: 180 feet
Lookout elevation: 5814 feet
Map: Green Trails Plain No. 146
GPS coordinates: N 47° 45' 43" W 120° 27' 58"
Permits and fees: None

GETTING TO THE TRAILHEAD

From US Highway 2 in Leavenworth, turn north onto State Route 209 (Chumstick Highway) and follow it for 2.1 miles. Turn right onto Eagle Creek Road and follow for 5.8 miles until the pavement changes to dirt. Turn left onto Forest Road 7520 and follow it for 5.9 miles to an intersection (with a bathroom available). Turn left on unmarked FR 5200, also called Entiat Summit Road, and drive 10.4 miles until you see a gravel road to the right. Park here on the side of the road. It's not an official trailhead but it's the easiest place to turn around. If you turn right, the road up ahead will be gated shortly.

There are two alternate approaches on the maze of forest roads in this area: the Chiwawa River valley and the Entiat Valley. This popular winter recreation area offers snowshoeing possibilities. Check with the local ranger district for current road conditions and accessibility.

Enjoy a short jaunt to a still-staffed lookout overlooking Leavenworth and pretty much all the eastern Central Cascades—and a major burn. There are alternate roads to get here; see the driving directions for details.

ON THE TRAIL

There are a ton of roads back here, and it's a popular area for mountain biking and cross-country skiing in the winter. It's possible to drive all the way to the summit, but only if the gate is open. If it's closed, there is not much room right at the gate to turn around, so it's best to park at the bottom of the turnoff (around 5630 feet) where there is plenty of space. Begin walking southeast up the road toward the lookout. At 0.1 mile, reach the large gate and walk around it. Continue walking up the gentle grade through burned conifers, including a lot of subalpine fir, from a 1994 burn (more on that later). Near the top, you'll pass some rocky side paths, possibly the lookout staffer's car in a gravelly lot, and a few benches before reaching the lookout at 0.5 mile and 5814 feet.

This is one of the few remaining lookouts still staffed in the Cascades. The official visiting hours here are 9:30 AM to 6:00 PM—remember that this is someone's home, even if just for a few months of the year. (There's no need to adhere to these hours in the off-season.) Wait until they invite you before you climb the stairs to the catwalk or go inside the lookout. The lookout staff work five to seven days per week, depending on fire conditions.

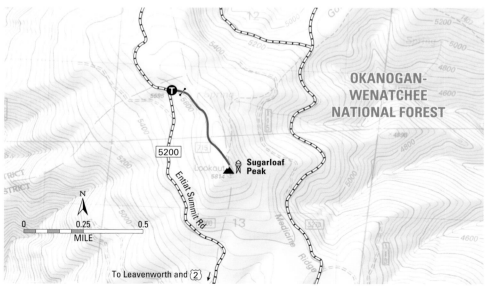

Sugarloaf Peak Lookout

Even though it's a short walk, don't assume the summit will be short on views. In fact, this is an absolutely breathtaking vantage point, and well worth a detour the next time you are in the Leavenworth area. Look south down to Leavenworth and the Wenatchee River. To the southwest, take in Big Jim Mountain, the Stuart Range, Cashmere Mountain, and the Enchantment Peaks. To the northwest, peer into the

Bench, burn, and view toward Entiat from Sugarloaf Peak

Chiwawa River valley, with the dense cluster of North Cascades peaks behind and Glacier Peak dominating the horizon. Southeast, you look toward Wenatchee and the Columbia River.

Sugarloaf Peak has been used as a lookout site since 1914. The first structure was a cupola, replaced by the L-4 cab you see today. The structure was built in 1933 on a different site and moved to Sugarloaf in 1949. The grounding infrastructure for lightning is in great condition, so make sure to check out the rods on the roof and the thick, braided-copper cables running from eaves down into the ground.

Sugarloaf is special not only because it's staffed, but also because it has two "sister" lookouts still visible. One is Alpine Lookout on Nason Ridge, which is 16 miles to the west. Alpine is also still staffed, making these the *only two remaining sister lookouts in operation in the Cascades*—meaning they could communicate with each other to triangulate on a fire, if needed. When I talked to these two lookout staffers, they told me they had spoken many times over the radio but had never met in person. How sweet is that?

The other sister lookout is on Tyee Mountain, 8 miles to the northeast. Tyee is no longer staffed, but looking north and northeast into the Entiat Range, you see evidence of the devastating Tyee Creek Fire of 1994, and how close it came to Sugarloaf. That fire was the second major threat to the structure, set in the heart of a burn-prone area. The first was the Entiat Experimental Forest Fire of 1970. In 1994, the staffer was rescued from the lookout by a fire crew, but the garage and outhouse burned down.

What caused such a massive burn? It was a perfect storm of conditions: There had been a drought for nearly a decade, and the wood had a very low moisture content. There was also still a lot of downed debris and fuel remaining from the huge 1970 fire that fueled the blaze in 1994. Temperatures reached the nineties in late June, and it stayed hot for the next month, with record-breaking highs regularly passing one hundred degrees. On July 24, a dry lightning storm rolled in, and you can guess what happened next. Dozens of fires started, and fire crews were able to fight some of them, but did not have the human labor or resources to stop them. Read more about the Tyee Creek Fire in Hike 27.

Return the way you came.

27 TYEE MOUNTAIN

YEAR CONSTRUCTED	LOOKOUT ACCESS	LOCATION
1952	Closed to public; catwalk accessible	Okanogan-Wenatchee National Forest, Entiat Ranger District

Roundtrip distance: 6.6 miles
Elevation gain: 1530 feet
Lookout elevation: 6654 feet
Map: Green Trails Brief No. 147
GPS coordinates: N 47° 50' 38" W 120° 29' 58"
Permits and fees: None

GETTING TO THE TRAILHEAD

From US Highway 97 in Entiat, turn west onto Entiat River Road. Pass the town of Ardenvoir at 9.5 miles. At approximately 10 miles, turn left onto Mad River Road. Continue for 2 miles and stay straight to get on Forest Road 5700 (instead of curving left for FR 5800). Starting mileage from here, follow the road, which is uphill and narrow, but paved. You pass Pine Flat Campground at 1.7 miles, as well as plenty of dispersed-campsite pullouts along this whole road. At around 7 miles, the road will

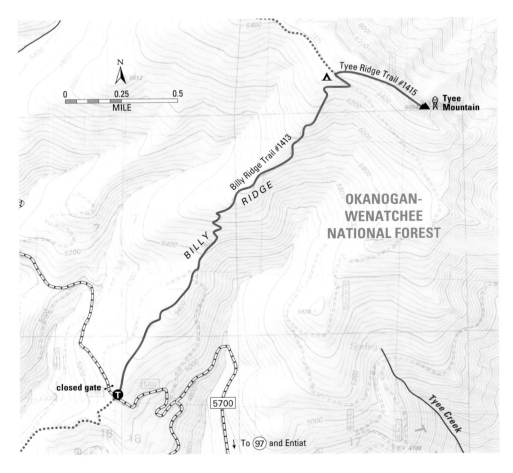

start dropping downhill. At 12.2 miles stay left, and the pavement ends and the surface becomes gravel. This is still FR 5700, though it is unmarked. At 14 miles, stay to the right to go uphill. You will reach a closed gate at 14.6 miles. Park here, without blocking the gate. The trailhead is signed where the Billy Ridge Trail intersects this road.

A way-off-the-beaten-track hike on the east side of the Cascades wanders through one of the biggest burns in recent decades.

ON THE TRAIL
Pick up Billy Ridge Trail #1413 where it intersects with the road. The signboard reminds you that this is a multiuse trail and to watch for bicycles, motorbikes, and

horses. Head northeast from the road on the narrow, sandy path. You will be in dappled shade as small pines and firs line the trail, along with tall grasses, lupine, fireweed, currant, and yarrow. At just over a tenth of a mile, catch a glimpse of the lookout—up and to the northeast.

At 0.25 mile, you'll start to see remnants of the 1994 Tyee Creek Fire. Here, the forest is mostly green, dotted with burned stumps and fallen, black logs and scarred trunks. But in 300 more feet, it gets grimmer—a forest graveyard, with many lifeless, bony-white trees down and dead ones creaking in the wind. The 1994 fire was catastrophic, and this is just the beginning of what you will see resulting from it.

Catch a little shade again at 0.6 mile as the forest fills in over you, and the trail briefly drops downhill before resuming an uphill climb at 1 mile. The good news is that with even a little elevation increase, the views begin to open up. Pretty brown-and-green foothills abound, and larger, snowy peaks of the Central Cascades start to show themselves to the west and southwest.

At 1.8 miles and 5800 feet enjoy an open, ridgelike grassy meadow. Wow. It's a flat landscape out to the east toward Chelan and beyond, with hills and mountains to the south. And just above you to the northeast is a great view of the lookout. With all the dead trees in these surrounding hills, you start to get a keener sense of the extent of the burn.

At 2.2 miles you go uphill again, but it's a pretty climb. It's also likely to be a hot one if you go in summer. Bring plenty of water and protection from the scorching

Looking back down the trail on the way to Tyee Mountain

Tyee Mountain Lookout

sun. The trail comes to a T intersection with an access road at 2.8 miles and around 6350 feet; turn left and walk on the road. In about 200 feet, you'll see a campsite on your left and the junction with Tyee Ridge Trail #1415. Stay right (east) with the curve of the road, and by 3.2 miles, you can see views over the ridge to the north. The road ends in a gravel parking area. Follow the trail to your left a few more steps to reach the lookout at 3.3 miles.

Welcome to a bygone era. Ascend 11 wooden steps to reach the catwalk. This is a great place to take in the views, though the lookout itself is not open—the door is locked, and the shutters are closed and secured with a cable. Between the severely peeling paint and the tarp poking out under the shutters on the west side, it's clear that this lookout has not gotten as much love (or funding) as it deserves. No one maintains it, and there are not any repair plans in the works.

To the southeast, take in the layers upon layers of dry hills—many ridges and drainages running perpendicular to the Entiat River valley. Sugarloaf is a sister lookout, 8 miles southwest. The summit area has a few small trees and a wild, windswept feel. There is ample flat space if you want to hang out, though it's unlikely that you will need that space, as this lookout seems to be seldom visited. South and downhill of the parking area is a privy in pretty rough shape, essentially unusable, with holes in the concrete floor.

This site has been used as a lookout since the first L-4 cab was built in 1931. The current hip-roofed L-4 fourteen-foot-by-fourteen-foot ground house with catwalk was built in 1952. There is a cold box on the north (shady) side of the building. A lot of local rock is used in the foundation—an unusual feature that you can also see at Sourdough and Alpine lookouts. The concrete feet were poured at varied levels on top of the stones to make the base level.

Tyee Mountain Lookout made national headlines in July 1994 when it reported the Tyee Creek Fire. I spoke to the Sugarloaf Peak and Mount Leecher lookouts' staff and a Steliko firefighter, and they all mentioned the impact of the Tyee Creek Fire—how much it changed the landscape around Entiat and Leavenworth. The fire started on July 24, 1994, when lightning struck in several places along Tyee Creek, an area that had been burned in the 1970 fires, and still had a lot of debris on the forest floor to fuel this fire. Crews responded immediately and in the dark but had to pull back due to dangerous conditions. It was extremely windy, and the fire jumped the Entiat River and Entiat River Road.

This devastating fire burned 180,000 acres over thirty-three days before it was contained, destroying thirty-five homes and cabins and the Tyee Mountain Lookout's outhouse. Other fires in the region on Hatchery Creek and Rat Creek consumed another 40,000 acres. Many structures were saved thanks to the efforts of firefighters and by the fire prevention strategies of homeowners. More than 2500 firefighters worked on the fire lines, and approximately 1000 US Marines from Camp Pendleton, in Southern California, were added to the effort. As of 2016, it stands as the eleventh-largest fire in Washington State history.

This area had originally been covered with ponderosa pine, which has a thick, fire-resistant bark. Periodic fires were essential to the trees' life cycles and for burning off small trees and brush. When the pine was harvested, Douglas fir, which is less resistant to fire, grew in its place. Some would point to the Tyee Creek Fire as a prime example of ineffective twentieth-century fire prevention—namely, the aggressive fire suppression policies of the state, the US Forest Service, and landowners that contributed to an uncharacteristic buildup of debris on the forest floor.

Return the way you came.

28 GRANITE MOUNTAIN

YEAR CONSTRUCTED	LOOKOUT ACCESS	LOCATION
1956	Closed to public	Mount Baker–Snoqualmie National Forest, Snoqualmie Ranger District

Roundtrip distance: 8 miles
Elevation gain: 3800 feet
Lookout elevation: 5629 feet
Map: Green Trails Snoqualmie Pass No. 207
GPS coordinates: N 47° 23' 52" W 121° 29' 11"
Permits and fees: Northwest Forest Pass required for parking at trailhead; self-register at trailhead for day-use hiking permit

GETTING TO THE TRAILHEAD

From Seattle, take Interstate 90 eastbound to exit 47 and turn left. Cross over the freeway and you'll reach a T intersection. Turn left (unmarked Forest Road 9034) and drive 0.3 mile to the trailhead. On a busy day, you will see cars parked on the side of the road well before the trailhead. Take care getting in and out of the space. Privy available. There is car camping available at Denny Creek Campground, also off exit 47 and 2.5 miles west of the exit.

> Good choice! There is almost nowhere else you can go for this much view, quad burning, and company. As the closest fire lookout to Seattle, it's no wonder it's so popular—try to visit on a weekday if you can.

ON THE TRAIL

Granite Mountain and Pratt Lake share the same trailhead. Don't forget to use the privy, as this often-switchbacking trail offers no privacy once you start hiking.

The trail starts out wide and gentle. It's a slow incline into the densely forested woods, with sounds of Interstate 90 still audible. At about a half mile in, you'll pass through an opening of fern and thimbleberries and be able to look up a huge, steep clearing. Back into the trees, at 1 mile you reach a trail junction. Straight would

Granite Mountain Lookout

take you toward Pratt and Talapus lakes. Take a hard right (northeast), following the sign for Granite Mountain.

Now the trail begins to climb. For the next mile and a half, be ready for steep switchbacks that dance between the forest and the clear gully you saw earlier. In winter, this is prime avalanche terrain. In summer, it's a sunny, challenging section that makes you look forward to the shaded parts. This is a good trail for trekking poles as it's steep, rocky, and varied. In just over a mile and a half, you ascend nearly 1800 vertical feet.

Then the views start to open up at 2.6 miles. You have a sweeping view south to Mount Rainier. You'll want to admire the vista, but remember to watch your feet; it starts to get really rocky here. The trails through this section also become a bit maze-like with little deviations—do your best to follow the main trail and not reinforce any shortcuts, which cause trail and habitat erosion.

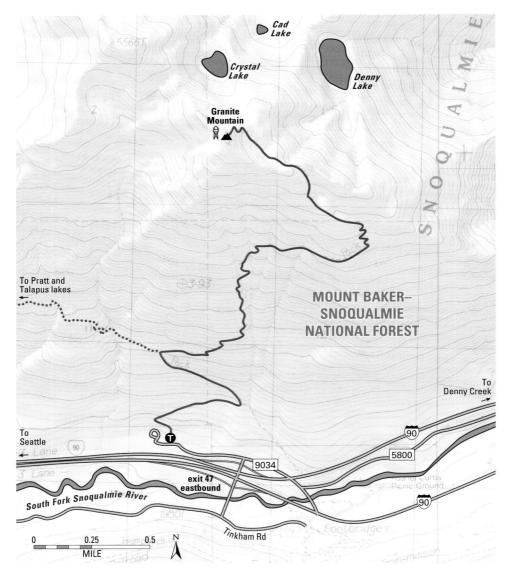

Just before 3 miles you'll reach a serene meadow of ferns, western anemones, blueberries, and a dappling of hemlock. The trail levels a bit, and you get your first view of the lookout. Now at 3.1 miles and 4850 feet, it feels like you have stepped into a subalpine meadow deep in the Cascades, even though you could see I-90 just a few minutes ago. Enjoy the flatness as the trail wraps around the north side of the ridge, below the lookout.

Now there is one last push at 3.7 miles and 5300 feet. You leave the meadows and start ascending steeply, on stone stairs in several spots. As you near the summit, the dirt trail will disappear, and you will be walking on a pile of granite rocks, confirmation of how aptly named the peak is. Proceed carefully on these stones of varying sizes. You reach the lookout at 4 miles and 5629 feet, with views in all directions. There is more space to sit on the east side of the lookout, and it is possible to walk around all sides of it, but unfortunately not onto the deck itself. The lookout is closed to the public and no longer staffed—unless you happen to be there at an odd time when a ranger stops by.

The structure you see is at least the third building on Granite Mountain. There was a cabin by 1920, a cupola by 1924, and both were still standing side by side in 1926. The current one, a fourteen-foot L-4 cab on a tower, replaced both when it was built in 1956.

Granite Mountain has been a tourist destination since cars could reach the campground at nearby Denny Creek. Even hikers without cars or driver's licenses could take the train—it would stop just west of the summit tunnel above Denny Creek. Sadly this is no longer possible, as this train route is no longer active.

According to Ira Spring and Byron Fish in *Lookouts*, the building is now stewarded by the Washington State Hi-Lakers, who adopted Granite Mountain Lookout in 1985 and contribute many hours of maintenance per year.

Return the way you came.

Hardware at Granite Mountain

29 THORP MOUNTAIN

YEAR CONSTRUCTED	LOOKOUT ACCESS		LOCATION
1930	Closed to public; staffed as needed		Okanogan-Wenatchee National Forest, Cle Elum Ranger District

Roundtrip distance: 7 miles (or 9.8-mile loop option)
Elevation gain: 2290 feet
Lookout elevation: 5854 feet
Map: Green Trails Kachess Lake No. 208
GPS coordinates: N 47° 22' 23" W 121° 50' 33"
Permits and fees: Northwest Forest Pass to park at trailhead

GETTING TO THE TRAILHEAD

From Seattle, take Interstate 90 eastbound to exit 80, signed for Roslyn and Salmon la Sac. Head north on Salmon la Sac Road (State Route 903) for 16.3 miles, passing through Roslyn and past Cle Elum Lake. You will pass official Wenatchee National Forest campgrounds along the lake at 10.6 miles (Wish Poosh Campground) and 16 miles (Cle Elum River Campground). Just past the upper end of the lake, turn left onto French Cabin Road (Forest Road 4308). Drive 3.2 miles and then turn right onto

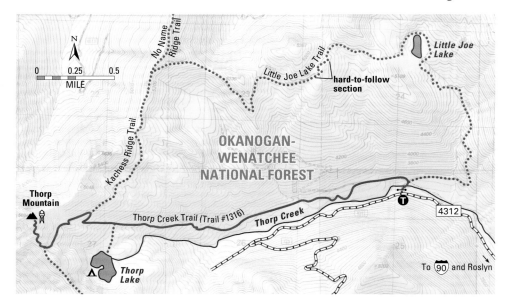

Hikers take in the view from Thorp Mountain Trail.

FR 4312, signed for Thorp Lake Trail. Continue 1.4 miles to another road junction. Park here on FR 4312, not blocking the gate on the decommissioned road to the right (north). There are places to camp all along the forest roads on the way in.

There is a completely different option for this route via the north side; for more information, look up the Kachess Ridge No Name Ridge Trail #1315 and Thorp Mountain Trail #1315.2.

> This pleasant, river-corridor hike (that bumps steeply upward to Kachess Ridge) heads to a historic, original 1930s lookout for peering north into the Glacier Peak Wilderness. Plus, you have the option of a longer loop hike.

ON THE TRAIL

There is a plastic marker on the right (north) side of the road for Trail #1316 (Thorp Creek Trail), and a low, rusty gate. Walk past the gate and almost immediately you will cross Thorp Creek. It looks like there used to be a bridge, but now you will need to carefully cross on rocks. In 0.1 mile, you reach a trail junction on what feels like an old logging road—very open, flat, and wide. You're going left (west) on Thorp Creek Trail #1316, but if you were to go right toward Little Joe Lake you would also eventually reach the lookout via a (much) longer loop option.

The beginning of the trail is like walking up a rocky, dry creekbed that is hemmed in tightly on both sides with vegetation. Thimbleberry, vine maple, Ceanothus, and hemlock are all around, and if the season is right, you can graze on blueberries as well. The grade is fairly flat as you parallel Thorp Creek, which you will hear off to your left. You'll start to gain elevation at 0.7 mile, crossing several smaller creeks as

Thorp Mountain Lookout

the trail alternates between gentle inclines and bigger bumps upward. By 1.5 miles, you are on a steady incline. By 1.9 miles the dense understory thins and opens up a bit, and although you can still hear the creek, you feel that you are moving up away from it.

At 2 miles, a huge fallen log has slightly shortened where the switchback used to go. Don't cross the log; there is now a steep path on this side of the tree up the flower-flecked hillside. Once you are above that section, the view and tree cover start to open up a little. At 2.4 miles and around 4770 feet, you reach a trail junction; stay straight (rightish) on the Thorp Mountain Trail #1315.2. (Going left here would take you to Thorp Lake in approximately a third of a mile, where there are four campsites, available on a first-come, first-served basis.) Not long after reaching this junction, you will reach another at 2.8 miles—the Kachess Ridge Trail. Go left. This is where you could opt to return via a loop hike toward Little Joe Lake, which adds nearly 3 extra miles, though.

Past here, you may encounter snow into July. You reach one more trail junction at 3.2 miles. Stay straight to continue to Thorp Mountain (going left takes you to Knox Creek). Now you know you are really getting up onto Kachess Ridge. This last little bit puts you in a beautiful meadow, with many wildflowers in the summer. In 1945 and 1946, the lookout was staffed by a schoolteacher who gathered and dried the flowers that she found on Thorp Mountain. By the end of the summer, she had identified ninety-two varieties of plants, and her collection was put on display for many years at the Cle Elum Ranger Station.

These beautiful meadows and growing views just add to the anticipation of what's to come. Unlike some lookouts that you can spot on a distant summit or ridge, Thorp doesn't show itself until just before you have arrived. Reach the lookout at 3.5 miles and 5854 feet. The 1930 L-4 ground house has a partial catwalk, wrapping around two and half sides. In the summer of 2007, the lookout was restored to the point of habitability, and is now staffed on an as-needed basis. It is on the National Historic Lookout Register.

Due west you can see Little Kachess Lake, the upper arm of the Kachess Lake reservoir. To the east is Cle Elum Lake. Southeast is Thorp Lake. Mount Stuart and Dragontail Peak are to the northeast, and Mount Rainier, to the southwest.

Return the way you came, or stay on the Kachess Ridge Trail toward Little Joe Lake to do a long loop. From here, it is 6 miles back to the trailhead via Little Joe Lake, instead of 3.2 miles to return the way you came. There is a section on the Little Joe Lake route where the trail becomes hard to follow. Research this option before you try it.

30 RED TOP MOUNTAIN

YEAR CONSTRUCTED	LOOKOUT ACCESS	LOCATION
1952	Open to public during business hours when staffed by volunteers; otherwise, locked at catwalk trapdoor	Okanogan-Wenatchee National Forest, Cle Elum Ranger District

Roundtrip distance: 1 mile (or 1.2-mile loop option)
Elevation gain: 330 feet
Lookout elevation: 5361 feet
Maps: Green Trails Mt. Stuart No. 209 and Liberty No. 210
GPS coordinates: N 47° 17' 50" W 120° 45' 36"
Permits and fees: Northwest Forest Pass to park at trailhead

GETTING TO THE TRAILHEAD

From Seattle, head east on Interstate 90 and take exit 85. Turn left (north) at the stop sign and proceed across the overpass, turning right in 0.4 mile onto State Route 970 East toward Wenatchee. Continue for 16.6 miles (SR 970 East will turn into US Highway 97 North). Just past Mineral Springs Campground, turn left onto Forest Road 9738. Continue for 2.6 miles, then veer left onto FR 9702, following the sign for Red Top Mountain. Follow FR 9702 for 4.5 miles until the road ends at a parking lot. Privy available. Car camping permitted at trailhead.

> This short, steep, and rewarding hike reaches a lookout staffed by a volunteer, with the option of a loop trail. You could volunteer here, too! It's a popular rock-hounding location as well.

ON THE TRAIL

This is a long parking lot. You can park sooner and be closer to the privy and trailhead signboard, or drive a little farther (north) and be closer to the start of the trail, the car-camping sites, and the circular turnaround. The trail starts on a wide path, and you can almost immediately see the lookout ahead to the north and 300 vertical feet above you.

This section of trail is flat and open, with views to the west and flowers underfoot, such as Nuttall's larkspur, which likes the gravelly slopes on the east side of the Cascades, as well as lupine and aster. In 0.2 mile, enter the shade of the woods where

Views of the Stuart Range from trail on Red Top Mountain

you will reach a signed junction with Teanaway Ridge Trail #1364. Right is signed for agate beds in 1 mile, and you can come back down from that direction. But for the shortest way to the lookout, stay left. You will ascend 300 feet in the next 0.3 mile. Enjoy this short, shady section in the trees. Wildflowers carpet the gravelly, clayish-soil slope. You'll start traversing the slope below the lookout as peaks come into view to your left (northwest) and ahead of you to the north.

At 0.4 mile, you reach an adorable outhouse. I know those two words typically do not go together, but this narrow, A-frame structure surrounded by flowers and punctuated with peaks behind it feels like an idyllic pit stop in the Alps—and is still usable.

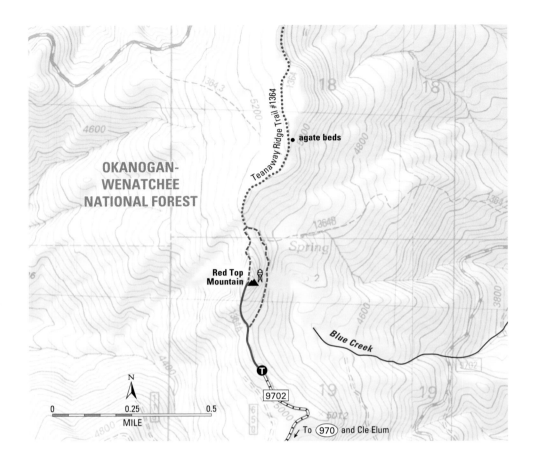

You reach the lookout in 0.5 mile at 5361 feet. If the lookout is not staffed, it will be locked at the deck trapdoor, and unfortunately the catwalk will be inaccessible. You can still take in phenomenal views from the ground. A sign informs visitors that pets are prohibited on the tower, and there is a maximum occupancy of six people. If the lookout is staffed, it is open to visitors from 9:00 AM to 6:00 PM. You can talk to the volunteer fire watcher and see the inside if you are invited. The cabin is cozy: a double bed with sheets, counters, a cribbage board, and the ubiquitous firefinder.

And *you* can be a volunteer fire watcher here for a day or two, too! If you're interested, contact the Cle Elum Ranger Station in February or March. The US Forest Service holds a mandatory one-day training session in May or June to bring its volunteers up to speed on their duties in fire detection, meeting and greeting visitors, and explaining history. Volunteers serve for one full day or can choose to serve two days and stay overnight.

The summit area has large, unique rock formations. It also has a solar panel and a huge antenna, which is an eyesore, but is necessary for the radio repeater to transmit signals. The views from the summit are a cool mix, from the rolling, green foothills to the east to the towering, glaciated peaks of Mount Stuart and the Stuart Range to the north and northwest. To the northeast are the Chelan and Entiat mountains. Nearby to the south is Teanaway Ridge. Mount Adams, Mount Rainier, and the city of Cle Elum are to the southwest. You can see toward the town of Ellensburg and the wind turbines to the southeast. Gaze westward, back toward bigger peaks near Snoqualmie Pass, looking beyond the outhouse and down the Middle Creek drainage which flows into the North Fork Teanaway River.

The earliest structure on this site was a cabin from 1924. Four years later, a D-6 cupola was built. Both of those buildings are gone, and today there stands a classic L-4 cab on a ten-foot tower from 1952. The structure was not used consistently and by the 1990s was showing its decades of being weatherworn. The Friends of Red Top Mountain, together with the Cle Elum Ranger District, undertook a two-year

Privy on trail to Red Top Mountain

Red Top Mountain Lookout

restoration effort that culminated in the lookout being added to the National Historic Lookout Register in August 1997.

Not only is the lookout back in service for fire detection and providing public information, but it's also a popular rock-hounding site. The area about a mile north of Red Top Mountain is known for outcroppings of agates and geodes (including 350-million-year-old jasper geodes). Rock collectors can find gold, geodes, and agates, including Ellensburg blue, an agate that is much sought after for its scarcity, range of color, and hardness, and found only near Ellensburg, Washington. You are allowed to collect materials for personal use and in small quantities—meaning one backpack or one five-gallon bucket per visit—and only for plant and invertebrate fossils. Commercial collectors or anyone collecting vertebrate fossils must obtain a permit.

You can return the way you came, or descend a different way on a loop trail, which adds just 0.2 mile to the return hike (for a total of 1.2 miles instead of 1 mile). To make the trail a loop, hike north from the lookout toward the large rock at the end of the ridge. Veer right at the fork in the trail (straight would put you going north on the Teanaway Ridge Trail and toward the agate beds), and descend on switchbacks along the eastern slope of Red Top Mountain. There are also some steep, rocky sections with a narrow trail, so use extra caution if you decide to descend this route. After about a half mile, you arrive at the junction with Teanaway Ridge Trail #1364 (mentioned earlier). Stay left to return to the parking lot.

SOUTH

31 KELLY BUTTE

YEAR CONSTRUCTED	LOOKOUT ACCESS	LOCATION
1950	Open to public for day use; overnight-volunteer staffing	Mount Baker–Snoqualmie National Forest, Snoqualmie Ranger District

Roundtrip distance: 3.2 miles
Elevation gain: 1050 feet
Lookout elevation: 5413 feet
Map: Green Trails Lester No. 239
GPS coordinates: N 47° 9' 47" W 121° 31' 31"
Permits and fees: Northwest Forest Pass to park

GETTING TO THE TRAILHEAD

From Greenwater, travel southeast about 2 miles on State Route 410. Turn left onto paved Forest Road 70. At 8.2 miles, turn left onto FR 7030, and then the pavement

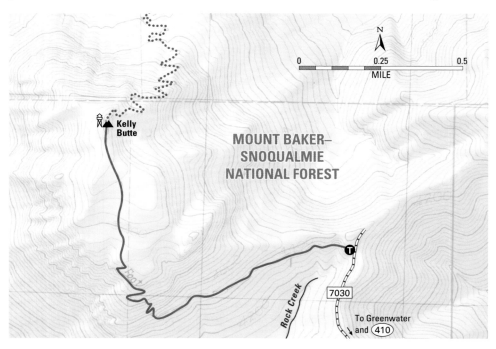

Kelly Butte Lookout with Mount Rainier in the distance

ends. At 8.5 miles cross a bridge and pass some campsites. At 12.3 miles, come to a T intersection and turn left, staying on unsigned FR 7030. A right turn will take you toward Colquhoun Peak, Pyramid Creek, and the Pacific Crest Trail (PCT). The rest of FR 7030 has a couple of steep sections and falling rock areas. At 12.8 miles go straight (not right and uphill).

At 13.5 miles turn right to stay on FR 7030 (signed). Pass side roads at 14 and 14.6 miles. The rough road to the Kelly Butte trailhead is on your left at 14.8 miles from SR 410. It's a small, makeshift trailhead parking area; park carefully to ensure other cars can exit easily. You will pass a lot of camping and target-practice pullout spots on the drive in. Due to the condition of the road, this area is inaccessible in winter.

> Enjoy a short climb to an unlocked lookout just outside Mount Rainier National Park, where you still get all the benefits of being close to the mountain with fewer crowds.

ON THE TRAIL

First, don't neglect the views from the trailhead parking lot. Take in the sight of Mount Rainier to the southwest and the lookout itself, a little dot up on the ridge to the northwest. Both will only get grander and closer, respectively. Start at the west end of the parking lot and walk west, continuing on an old logging road. It's wide and flat. The Douglas firs shade you, and phlox, lupine, wild strawberries, and ferns line the way.

At 0.7 mile, hop off the nice flat road and take a hard right (north) onto a trail. Now the path barrels uphill unrelentingly—get ready to go up more than 600 feet in less than half a mile. It puts you onto a steep, rocky hillside, cluttered with rocks of various sizes and many wildflowers, like Indian paintbrush, kinnikinnick, magenta-colored rock penstemon, and thimbleberry. Even though this section is relatively short, bring plenty of water for this steep, shadeless climb. Across the way, take in the other foot-hills crisscrossed by logging roads. At just under 1 mile, you will pass under a rock face with sport-climbing bolts. If you want to combine a lookout hike with a little rock climbing, this is the trail for you!

At 1.1 miles and around 5120 feet, the hillside switchbacks end, and the trail straightens and heads north on a flatter grade. You're on a wide ridgeline, and soon get huge views to your left (west) and right (northeast) and even a glimpse of the lookout ahead.

Continue on until you reach the lookout at 1.6 miles, and gape at the imposing Mount Rainier to the south. Take a spin around the 360-degree catwalk and feast on the mountains to the north, from left to right (west to east): Kaleetan and Chair peaks, Granite Mountain, Denny Mountain, Snoqualmie Mountain, Glacier Peak, Mount Thompson, Alaska Mountain, Huckleberry Mountain, Chikamin Ridge, and Hibox Mountain. And in the foreground, a lot of clear-cutting.

The first structure at this site was a cupola cabin erected in 1926. Today there stands an L-4 cab built in 1950, and staffed until the 1980s. The lookout was renovated

Views of Mount Rainier from trail to Kelly Butte

Hiker and views from summit of Kelly Butte

by volunteers, with completion in September 2011. (It is sometimes staffed by volunteers; if you're interested, contact the ranger district for details.) Otherwise the structure is open to the public, and you can check out the inside, with the original firefinder stand and glass-foot-insulated stool. There are also two cots, a few chairs, a first-aid kit, broom, and a table with visitor logbooks dating back to 2008.

Keep an eye out for elk and mountain goats. Return the way you came.

32 SUN TOP

YEAR CONSTRUCTED	LOOKOUT ACCESS	LOCATION
1933	Staffed by volunteers in summer; accessible to public when invited in by staff	Mount Baker–Snoqualmie National Forest, Snoqualmie Ranger District

Roundtrip distance: 1 mile
Elevation gain: 450 feet
Lookout elevation: 5271 feet
Map: Green Trails Greenwater No. 238
GPS coordinates: N 47° 2' 13" W 121° 24' 11"
Permits and fees: None

GETTING TO THE TRAILHEAD

From State Route 410 just east of Milepost 49, turn east on Forest Road 73 and go 1.3 miles. There is a Sno-Park lot here where you would park in winter; pass required. In summer, turn left here onto FR 7315 and follow it for another 5 miles to a large, flat forest road intersection area. Turn right and follow the road 0.1 mile to the access gate, and park on the side of the road. If it's crowded or you don't want to park on the slope, there is plenty of space in the large flat area just below.

A short hike or drive up offers a stunning view of Mount Rainier, especially of the Winthrop Glacier and the striking Willis Wall, and the option of snowshoeing in the winter.

ON THE TRAIL

In the winter this trip would be a hefty snowshoe of almost 6 miles and more than 3000 feet each way. But in the summer, you can drive nearly all the way to the summit. The gate may or may not be open, so expect to hike the half mile on the road or

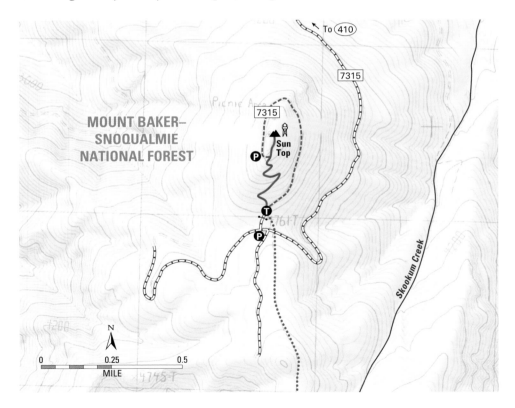

Sun Top Lookout

forested trail to get to the top. You can choose which route to take, or even turn this outing into a loop hike if you're willing to walk back down the road. But if the gate is open and cars are passing, it's best to stick to the trail and avoid the vehicle traffic.

To start in the woods, follow the signed trail to the left of the road in front of the gate. It's short, but it still takes some work—you're going up nearly 500 feet in half a mile. It's a pleasant, shady walk with moss draping from the tree branches. Pass western anemone, Oregon grape, and vanilla leaf on this narrow trail.

Get peekaboo views to the right (east) at 0.2 mile. By 0.25 mile, you can start to see the outer glaciers on Mount Rainier to the south if it's a clear day. By 0.45 mile you'll emerge onto the road and see the lookout up ahead. You'll come to a parking lot with a privy available. Just off the parking lot are two picnic tables, in case you want to stop. Continue following the path and reach the lookout at 0.5 mile and 5271 feet.

The L-4 ground house was built in 1933, but the road to it was not completed until 1956. It was briefly used as part of the Aircraft Warning Service during World War II. The building was reconstructed in 1990 and is listed on the National Historic Lookout Register.

Picnic area at Sun Top Mountain

It is currently staffed occasionally by volunteers in the summer. Depending on the day you're there, you may be able to see inside the lookout, or it may be completely locked up. If you're interested in being a volunteer, contact the ranger district for details.

A picnic table just past the lookout features an imposing view of Mount Rainier and a straight-on view of the Winthrop Glacier—a stellar place for a picnic or a rest. You can also see Mount Rainier's Willis Wall, a five-thousand-foot cliff, as well as the White River and Huckleberry Creek valleys. Mount Baker and Mount Stuart loom in the north. It's a lovely summit area in a sunny, open meadow with wildflowers, red-flower currant, and small evergreens mixed in.

Return the way you came, unless you strongly prefer walking back down the forest road for variety.

33 TOLMIE PEAK

YEAR CONSTRUCTED	LOOKOUT ACCESS	LOCATION
1934	Closed to public; catwalk open; staffed as needed by National Park Service	Mount Rainier National Park

Roundtrip distance: 5.6 miles
Elevation gain: 1000 feet
Lookout elevation: 5925 feet
Map: Green Trails Mt. Rainier West No. 269
GPS coordinates: N 46° 56' 14" W 121° 52' 04"
Permits and fees: Mount Rainier annual pass, NPS interagency pass, or per-car fee (good for up to seven days); Carbon River Ranger Station

GETTING TO THE TRAILHEAD

From Puyallup, drive east for 13 miles on State Route 410 to the town of Buckley. Turn right (south) onto SR 165 and follow it for 10.3 miles, passing through Carbonado and over the Fairfax Bridge. Bear right onto Mowich Lake Road. From here, the pavement will end at 5.4 miles, and you will cross the Mount Rainier National Park boundary at 14.9 miles. You reach the fee station at 15.6 miles—use the envelope provided to pay the day-use fee (valid for seven days), unless you have an approved pass. There are bathrooms and picnic tables at the fee station, but camping is prohibited.

Eunice Lake from trail to Tolmie Peak

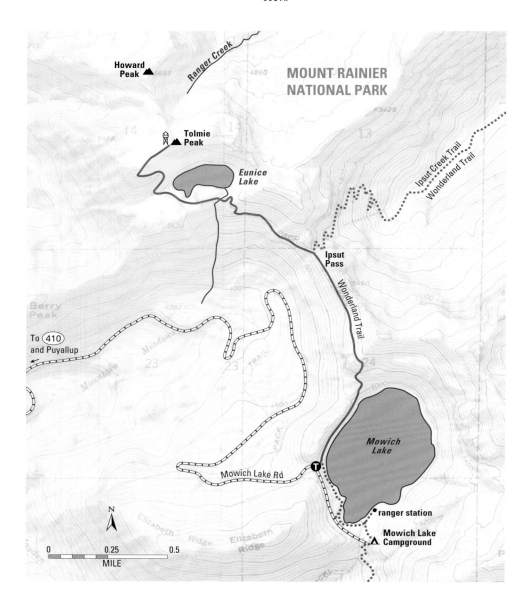

From here, the road gets a little rougher, and trailers are not advised. A high-clearance vehicle is not necessary, but would make the drive more comfortable. Continue on, reaching the Tolmie Peak Trailhead at 20.3 miles from the turnoff. It's on the left (northeast) side of the road. Parking is allowed only on one side of the road, and cars park on the side both before and after the trailhead. If you wanted to do a slightly longer hike, you could

LEFT *Park service ranger painting Tolmie Peak Lookout* **RIGHT** *Visitor logbook on catwalk of Tolmie Peak Lookout*

drive to the end of the road at Mowich Lake Campground. There is designated camping there, but overnight camping is prohibited at the lookout and Eunice Lake. Note that Mowich Lake Road is closed in winter.

This pretty, midlength day hike on the northwest side of Mount Rainier heads to an original 1930s lookout, with car-camping options and a gateway to other Carbon and Mowich area trails.

ON THE TRAIL

Start at the signed trailhead at 4929 feet. You get to hop on the iconic Wonderland Trail, a 93-mile loop that encircles Mount Rainier, for the beginning of the route. Mowich Lake sparkles a dark turquoise through the trees to your right (east), and Mowich Lake Campground, a walk-in (drivable too) campground is close by. The trail is shady as it heads north, hugging the lakeshore for the first 0.33 mile. Then it veers left away from the lake and starts climbing.

At 1 mile, you reach the junction with the Ipsut Creek Trail for Ipsut Pass to the right (north), which is where the Wonderland Trail goes. If you wanted to extend your

View up to Tolmie Peak from near Eunice Lake

trip to do some backpacking, this is a gateway to more backcountry in the national park as it wraps around the north side of the mountain. Stay left (west), signed for Eunice Lake and Tolmie Peak. From here, you descend on switchbacks for less than half a mile before you start going up again. Watch your step in this section; the trail is quite rooty and varied. There are pretty rock walls near the trail, including bits of columnar basalt, and when you emerge from the forest at 1.9 miles, you get your first view of the lookout up ahead on the ridge.

Now at around 5350 feet, Eunice Lake is on your right, with numerous spur trails that take you to the lakeshore. Camping is prohibited in the Eunice Lake basin, but it's a lovely area to explore if you have the time. The trail heads due west, following the south side of the lake for at least a third of a mile. At 2 miles, you cross a small creek—a possible water source if needed. Just beyond, you'll reach an open, almost beach-like section of the lake. While this serene spot may entice you toward the shore, make an effort to stay on the established trails as this area has a lot of fragile subalpine vegetation.

Once you reach the far west end of Eunice Lake, the trail turns north and starts to climb again. As you get higher, Mount Rainier seems to grow to the southeast. Press on for the final uphill push until you reach the ridgeline at 2.6 miles. Now you get views north to the other side, and probably some wind; you may need to add a layer here. But you've almost made it! Follow the ridge northeast until you arrive at the lookout at 2.8 miles.

Four sites (including Tolmie) had been used very early on for fire detection in the national park, but were rag camps, where the lookout staff lived in tents. It wasn't until the New Deal that the Park Service was able to put up structures on Tolmie, Mount Fremont, Gobblers Knob, and Crystal Peak. In 1934, as the CCC built trails and bridges, the Park Service put out a request for bids on the lookout buildings. A Seattle firm built the structures: four two-story, hip-roofed, fourteen-by-fourteen-foot lookouts with wraparound catwalks. Three of the four are still standing and in use (the exception being Crystal Peak) and on the National Register of Historic Places.

Tolmie has been partially rebuilt and could use a little more TLC, though it's in decent shape. You can go up on the catwalk for a 360-degree view, sign the logbook on the deck, peer inside the window, and see the original firefinder—but the door is locked. Gaze north into the Carbon River valley or south to looming Mount Rainier. Layer upon layer of green hills surround Tolmie, punctuated with rocky outcroppings and dramatic cliff faces.

If you eat any snacks at the top, be extremely careful to not drop crumbs, preventing further habituating animals to prowl this area for human food. It's already pretty bad; the gray jays (also known as whisky jacks) may dive-bomb you while you are holding food, or a chipmunk might jump onto you or into your backpack in search of treats. Keep any food that you are not eating at that moment covered, wrapped, or lidded.

Return the way you came.

34 MOUNT FREMONT

YEAR CONSTRUCTED	LOOKOUT ACCESS		LOCATION
1934	Closed to public; staffed as needed in summer by National Park Service		Mount Rainier National Park

Roundtrip distance: 5.6 miles

Elevation gain: 800 feet

Lookout elevation: 7181 feet

Map: Green Trails Mount Rainier Wonderland No. 269SX

GPS coordinates: N 46° 54' 56" W 121° 21' 22"

Permits and fees: Mount Rainier annual pass, NPS interagency pass, or per-car fee (good for seven days); White River Wilderness Information Center

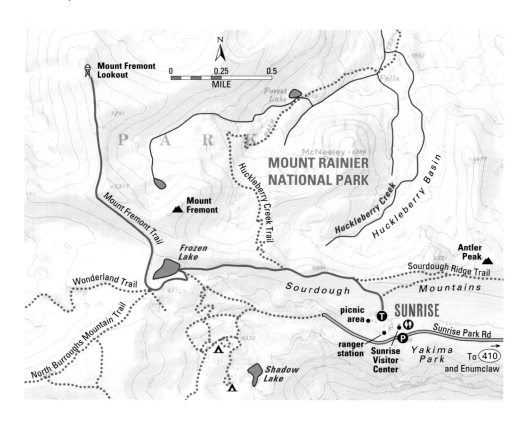

Morning alpenglow on Mount Rainier from Sunrise parking area trailhead

GETTING TO THE TRAILHEAD

From Enumclaw, follow State Route 410 east for 43 miles until you reach Sunrise Park Road (White River Road). Make a slight right at the fork and follow along for 5 miles, crossing the White River. The road then switchbacks to become exclusively Sunrise Park Road and continues 10 miles to its end at the Sunrise Visitor Center parking lot. To get to the trailhead, walk to the northwestern part of the parking lot to a picture of a hiker. Then you'll see a sign that says "Trail Access 600 feet," which marks the official beginning of the trail.

Sunrise makes for a unique trailhead. It's the highest point that can be reached by car in Mount Rainier National Park and has stunning views of the mountain. It also offers a ton of amenities. The Sunrise Visitor Center is open daily beginning in early July through early September and is closed in winter; it offers exhibits, guided interpretive programs, book sales, and a picnic area. The Sunrise Day Lodge is open from early July through late September, with food service and a gift shop. It does not offer overnight lodging.

Car camping is available 12 miles before Sunrise at the White River Campground. If you camp there and are feeling ambitious, you can get to Sunrise for its namesake and watch the alpenglow on Mount Rainier as the day begins.

Enjoy a relatively short and easy hike from the already spectacular Sunrise Visitor Center up to over 7000 feet elevation in the heart of the national park, with an up-close view of the northeastern flank of Mount Rainier.

ON THE TRAIL

Because this is a heavily visited area, there are a lot of trails and plenty of signage. Pay close attention to the map and at each trail junction to make sure you stay headed in the right direction.

Start in the Sunrise Visitor Center parking lot. At 6400 feet, mornings and evenings are going to be cold, and in late summer you might find hoarfrost, even when the air temperature is warm. Follow the sign with a picture of a hiker on the northwest side of the parking lot, and then another sign that says "Trail Access 600 feet."

The trail starts as a wide gravel path with open, grassy slopes and some small evergreen trees on either side. In about 500 feet, stay left at a trail junction, following the sign that says "1.3 miles to Fremont Trail."

Mount Fremont Lookout (photo by Kate Rogers)

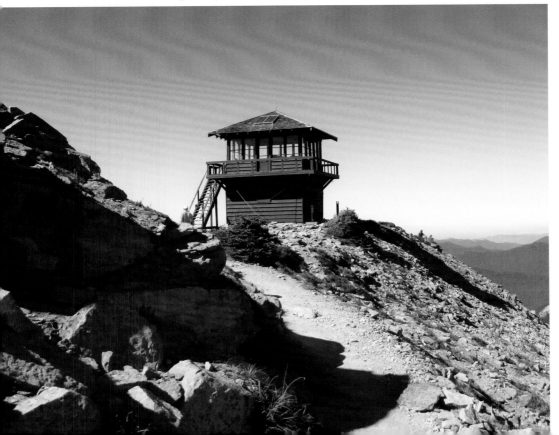

Hike up another 0.25 mile to another junction. You are now on the Sourdough Ridge Trail. Turn left toward the Huckleberry Creek Trail and Frozen Lake (at 1 mile). As you start ascending, you will see views of both Mount Baker and Glacier Peak to the north. At 0.6 mile, there is a slight split to the right for the Huckleberry Creek Trail; be sure to stay straight.

By 0.75 mile in, this is about as good as hiking gets in the Central Cascades. The trail is flat and forgiving, except for a tiny bit of scree to pick your way across at 0.8 mile. On a clear day, a stunning Mount Rainier will loom large to the southwest (your left) with long views to the south and east.

You reach a junction at 1.25 miles and go right toward Mount Fremont. At 1.5 miles is another junction, and this five-way trail intersection makes you feel like you are on a hiking superhighway! You could go left for the North Burroughs Mountain Trail or straight for the Wonderland Trail. But it's easy to navigate: just stay to the far right for the Mount Fremont Trail.

You'll see Frozen Lake to your right. From the map alone, I thought it might be a nice spot to take a dip on a hot day, but note that it's a roped-off reservoir and closed for swimming.

The trail slowly starts to climb again on an open slope. At 2 miles in, cross another small scree field. Far below, to your left, are a beautiful bowl valley and meadow. At just over 2 miles, you get your first glimpse of the lookout to the northwest, along with views of Puget Sound. The trail flattens as you traverse the last section.

Reach the summit in 2.8 miles. At 7181 feet, this is one of the highest lookouts in the state, and it has the views to prove it. The scenic expanse is almost 360 degrees, with just a slight view blockage by a ridge to the southeast. The lookout is closed to the public, but you can take in the panorama from the wraparound deck. It's a typical two-story Park Service construction, with a first floor for storage and the second floor a fourteen-by-fourteen-foot cab.

According to Ray Kresek in his book *Fire Lookouts of the Northwest*, no sooner was the lookout completed in 1934 than a gust of wind lifted it up and carried the entire second story over the cliff into Huckleberry Creek. Carpenters arrived the next day to add guy cables—but they took one look at the mess and walked off the job.

You can bet they did a better job securing the lookout after that, and it was staffed as an operational lookout through most of the twentieth century. Now it is nicely maintained by the Park Service and staffed on an as-needed basis during the summer season, after lightning storms or during known fires.

Return the way you came.

35 GOBBLERS KNOB

YEAR CONSTRUCTED	LOOKOUT ACCESS		LOCATION
1933	Closed to public; catwalk accessible; staffed as needed in summer by National Park Service		Mount Rainier National Park *Note: Trail starts west of the park boundary in Glacier View Wilderness.*

Roundtrip distance: 7 miles
Elevation gain: 1000 feet
Lookout elevation: 5485 feet
Map: Green Trails Mount Rainier Wonderland No. 269SX
GPS coordinates: N 46° 47' 46" W 121° 3' 8"
Permits and fees: Self-register for a free Wilderness Use Permit at the trailhead for day trips and overnights; Longmire Wilderness Information Center

GETTING TO THE TRAILHEAD

Follow State Route 706 east from Ashford for 3.8 miles then turn left (north) onto Forest Road 59 (Copper Creek Road). Note that this rough road may be challenging in a low-clearance vehicle. Check with the Wilderness Information Center (WIC) for current conditions. Continue 3.4 miles up this road to a junction, and stay left. Continue on, staying on the primary road. At 8.6 miles you will have a spectacular view of Mount Rainier on a clear day, as the road jogs to the right. Do not go right; stay straight as the road starts to descend. The road ends here and there is space for about ten cars to park at the trailhead for Glacier View Trail #267. There is a self-register station but no privy. There are plenty of pull-over spots for dispersed camping on the forest road in.

Deep in a fairly inaccessible corner of Mount Rainier National Park sits this pristinely restored lookout with a view of a towering, seldom-seen side of the mountain and good camping options just below. There are a couple of trailheads where you can begin this hike, both along the same forest road—Lake Christine Trail #249 is a shorter drive but slightly longer hike. I started at the trailhead for Glacier View Trail #267, which is a farther drive past Lake Christine, but puts you closer to the lookout to start. The two trails intersect well before the lookout.

OPPOSITE *Gobblers Knob Lookout from trail*

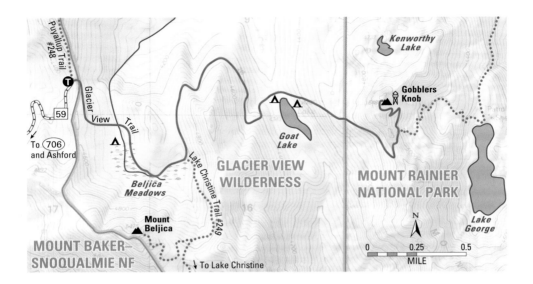

ON THE TRAIL

Once upon a time, in the 1980s, you could access a trailhead in the national park via the Westside Road to get to Gobblers Knob (in my opinion, the most colorfully named of all the state's lookouts). But due to routine washouts, the Westside Road has been closed to the public for decades, with no signs of ever reopening. That means there is no road into the park that puts you at the southwest corner of the mountain, and any of those views must be reached by trail. It also means you can't actually start this hike in the national park.

Instead, start at about 4500 feet at the Glacier View trailhead on the edge of the Glacier View Wilderness. After you self-register, start off on the forest trail. In a few hundred feet, the trail comes to a T intersection: right for Glacier View Trail or left for Puyallup Trail #248. Turn right. The trail is fairly narrow in this shady forest of hemlock and fir, and it's thick with blueberry bushes. Don't count on snacking on these, though—on one of my visits they had an unpleasant taste and looked a little blighted.

Soon the trail starts dropping toward Beljica Meadows. At 0.45 mile, you could veer right into the pretty meadow area, where there are campsites and views of Mount Beljica overhead. Stay on the main trail to continue down to 0.5 mile, where you will reach the low point of the trail and a stream at 4460 feet. It was still trickling when I was there in August of an incredibly dry and low-snow year, so it seems like a fairly safe bet for a water source should you need one in a pinch.

Now continue along the north side of Beljica Meadows, admiring its neat maze of waterways and tall, marshy grasses. All the standing water means this area is also very mosquito-prone, even into the dry time of late summer. At 1 mile, you reach the junction sign for the Lake Christine Trail #249 to the right (south), which leads to the alternate trailhead and is only slightly longer than this route.

Stay to the left (north) on the main trail as you continue to gently ascend. You'll leave the forest momentarily to pass through a flattish quarter-mile-long meadow of berries and evergreen saplings. At 2.2 miles, arrive at Goat Lake. There is one campsite, immediately to your right, or continue on the trail, which wraps around the north and east sides of the lake to find other camping options. At 2.7 miles, you reach the boundary for Mount Rainier National Park, with signs directing you toward Lake George, the Westside Road, and your choice, Gobblers Knob. Continue hiking in sunny, lush patches of thimbleberry until you reach a tiny saddle at 3.2 miles. Walk just another couple hundred feet as the trail descends briefly, and then take a hard left (north) on a signed trail. (Going straight would take you to the old Gobblers Knob trailhead on the Westside Road.)

Now you are almost there! Start climbing again, ascending approximately eight switchbacks toward the knob, with the dark brown side of the lookout coming into view, looking more like a vacation home at first glimpse than a utilitarian lookout.

Gobblers Knob Lookout

You reach the summit at 5485 feet and 3.5 miles. The lookout takes up almost the entire flat area that the small summit offers. It was built in 1933 in the distinct two-story design characteristic of the national park—the same as Tolmie Peak, Mount Fremont, and Shriner Peak. This one seems to be especially clean and well maintained, and had a new roof and floor installed in the last couple years. The building is closed to the public, but the catwalk is open, and it's an amazing spot for peering at the looming Mount Rainier. From this unique southwest corner vantage point, you can see intricacies of the Puyallup, Tahoma, and South Tahoma glaciers, plus the South Puyallup River and Tahoma Creek coming off the mountain, the Wonderland Trail, and numerous lakes, including Kenworthy Lake and Lake George directly below.

Return the way you came.

36 SHRINER PEAK

YEAR CONSTRUCTED	LOOKOUT ACCESS	LOCATION
1932	Closed to public; catwalk is open; staffed as needed in summer by National Park Service	Mount Rainier National Park

Roundtrip distance: 8.4 miles
Elevation gain: 3420 feet
Lookout elevation: 5834 feet
Map: Green Trails Mount Rainier Wonderland No. 269SX
GPS coordinates: N 46° 48' 8" E 121° 26' 42"
Permits and fees: Mount Rainier annual pass, NPS interagency pass, or day-use fee; additional backcountry permit for overnight stays; White River Wilderness Information Center

GETTING TO THE TRAILHEAD

From Enumclaw, drive east 47 miles on State Route 410 to SR 123. Turn right onto SR 123 (Cayuse Pass Highway), following signs for White River. Drive about 8 miles south of that junction to reach the parking area. There is parking on the right (west) side of the road immediately before the trailhead, which is on the left (east) side of the road.

The closest car camping in the park is at Ohanapecosh Campground to the south, and White River Campground to the northwest. Reservations are essential, as these campgrounds fill up well in advance in the summer.

Mount Rainier reflected in the windows of Shriner Peak Lookout

A quintessential Mount Rainier hike: get up close and personal with the mountain, enjoy grand vistas, graze on blueberries, and snag a primo place to camp.

ON THE TRAIL

From the road at about 2400 feet, start into a classic northwest forest of hemlock, fir, and cedar. As the trail climbs in the shade, you'll also spot vine maple, ferns, huckleberries, and Oregon grape. The trail is a soft duff and nice to walk on, but it wastes no time in going up. By 1 mile in, you've already gained about 750 feet. Now the trail trends northeast and you pass a few impressive old-growth stumps. At 1.5 miles you come out into the sun with views to the south and east. At 1.7 miles, the switchbacks begin, and you continue ascending. At 2.5 miles, the mountain first comes into view, and by 3.3 miles the trail gets noticeably steeper. There are a ton of blueberry bushes along the trail—enjoy continual grazing if you are there at the right time (usually late July and August). Continue moving in and out of the shade and sun until reaching the top at 4.2 miles. The view of Mount Rainier is luminous—providing, of course, that it's clear. Even if clouds cover the big mountain, the rest of the landscape will not disappoint.

The lookout is a two-story, fourteen-by-fourteen-foot wooden structure with catwalk that has not been staffed since the 1980s, but is still used by the Park Service on an as-needed basis. Mount Rainier National Park rangers will occasionally stay here in critical fire weather, or simply to interact with visitors and help ensure safety and leave-no-trace principles. When the lookout was built in 1932, a contractor packed in the materials all the way from the Chinook Pass Highway. Demonstrating a classic National Park Service design from the 1930s, it is the oldest of the four lookouts remaining in Mount Rainier National Park. The inside is closed to the public, but the catwalk is open.

There are also two designated campsites at the summit, just a short walk from the lookout. You must obtain a backcountry permit at the wilderness center prior to camping up there, and then display the permit on your tent. The privy is an open-air solar toilet—a clear plastic frontpiece uses passive solar gain to more quickly break down the waste. There is also a bear pole with a rod where you can easily hang your

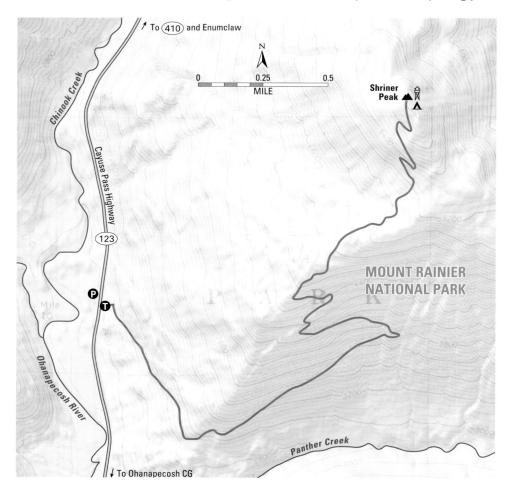

Shriner Peak Lookout and Mount Rainier

food and other scented items in a stuff sack; because of this feature, bear canisters are not required.

Return the way you came.

37 HIGH ROCK

YEAR CONSTRUCTED	LOOKOUT ACCESS	LOCATION
1930	Open to public for day use	Gifford Pinchot National Forest, Cowlitz Valley Ranger District

Roundtrip distance: 3 miles
Elevation gain: 1330 feet
Lookout elevation: 5685 feet
Map: Green Trails Randle No. 301
GPS coordinates: N 46° 39' 59" W 121° 6' 30"
Permits and fees: None

GETTING TO THE TRAILHEAD

From Elbe (about 40 miles south of Tacoma along State Route 7), follow SR 706 east for 10.1 miles. When you pass Ashford, it is approximately 2 more miles to your next turn,

High Rock Lookout

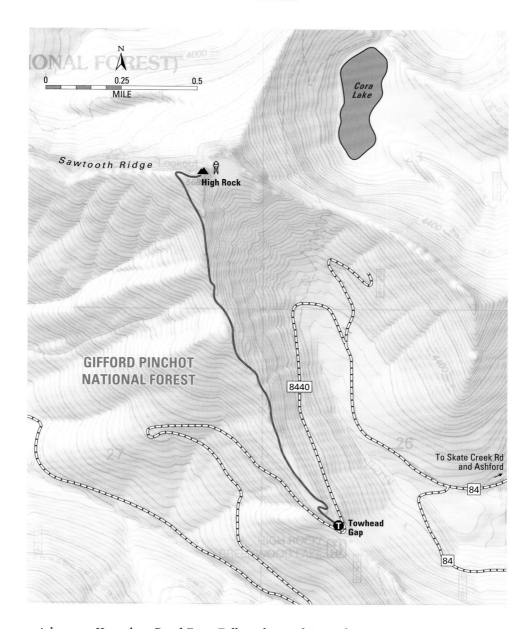

a right onto Kernahan Road East. Follow the road 1.4 miles. Here it curves to the left and becomes Skate Creek Road, which you follow for 3.3 miles. Turn right onto Forest Road 84, but note that the sign for FR 84 is not visible when approaching from this direction. At 1.5 miles you'll see a fork to the right for FR 8410. Stay left and continue

Mount Rainier from inside High Rock Lookout

on FR 84 for 6.8 miles. Stay right when it forks to transition to FR 8440 (though it is not signed). At 2.6 miles along FR 8440, the road levels off and gets broad enough to park a dozen or more vehicles. Park here; this is the trailhead at Towhead Gap.

High Rock and the lookout are visible from the east side of the parking area. Note that Towhead Gap is on a hairpin turn so take care where you park, as parked vehicles might not be visible to cars coming around the corner of the road. There are several pullouts along the length of FR 84 should you want to camp.

> South of Mount Rainier National Park, on the highest perch in the Sawtooth range, this cliffside lookout offers major bang for your buck—dramatic views of Mount Rainier with just a short hike in.

ON THE TRAIL

When this lookout was first built, hikers had to tackle more than 10 miles of trail and 4000 feet of elevation gain to get there. But don't worry—these days, with the expansion of logging in the area, it's less than 2 miles in. Find the trailhead at the northwest side of the parking area, to the left of a small sign. The trail starts out in the shade, and becomes a fairly steady climb right along a ridgeline. At 1 mile in,

OPPOSITE *High Rock Lookout on its high rock perch*

from a rocky outcropping to the side of the trail, you catch your first views of Mount Rainier and Mount Adams. Continue on and reach a collapsed cabin in the woods at 1.3 miles.

Then you'll emerge from the forest, and you're almost there, but the terrain changes to a rock slope. A faint trail continues, traversing the rock and skirting east before switching back and up toward the lookout. It is a good option, though some hikers opt for the more direct route of walking straight up the rocks. Either way, you will make it to the summit from the lookout's south side at 1.5 miles, with a dramatic 1600-foot drop to the east and north to Cora Lake. You get to take in views of Mounts Rainier, Adams, and St. Helens from the highest point in the Sawtooth range.

The lookout is one and a half stories with a three-sided deck, built in 1930—on the early side for the L-4 design. The inside is sparsely furnished, with a table, desk, and logbook for visitors to sign. The stand is still in the middle of the room, but the firefinder that once sat on it is gone. The lookout was staffed until at least 2007, and the building is now open to day-trippers, but overnight use is prohibited, as the structure is no longer properly grounded for lightning.

Return the way you came.

38 BURLEY MOUNTAIN

YEAR CONSTRUCTED	LOOKOUT ACCESS	LOCATION
1934	Open to public for day use during summer; locked in off-season	Gifford Pinchot National Forest, Cowlitz Valley Ranger District

Roundtrip distance: 15 miles
Elevation gain: 4020 feet
Lookout elevation: 5304 feet
Map: Green Trails McCoy Peak No. 333
GPS coordinates: N 46° 26' 18" W 121° 8' 53"
Permits and fees: None

GETTING TO THE TRAILHEAD

From US Highway 12 in Randle, drive 1 mile south on State Route 131 and then turn left (east) on Forest Road 23 (Cispus Road). Continue on FR 23 for 8.2 miles to its junction with FR 28. Bear right on FR 28, cross the Cispus River, and turn right in 1.3

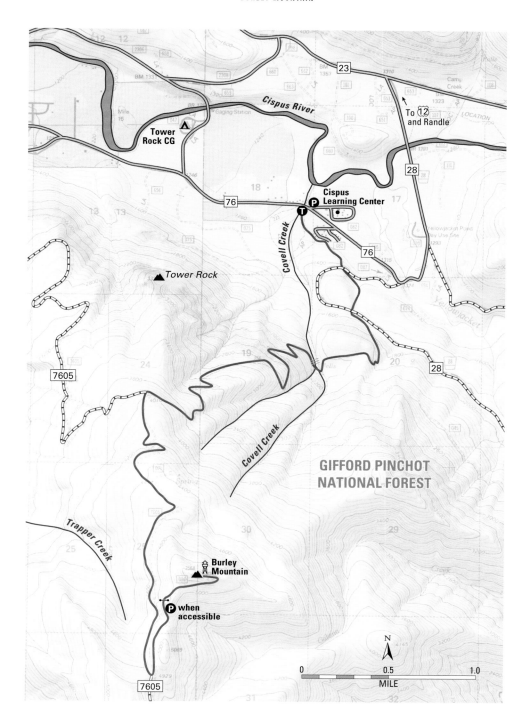

View from the trail to Burley Mountain

miles on FR 76. Continue for 0.6 mile until you reach the large sign on your right for the Cispus Learning Center. The trailhead is on the left side of the road, across from the Cispus sign, but there is no parking. To park, turn right into the Cispus Learning Center complex, and in about 400 feet you will see the visitor center on your right. Park in the lot on your left across from the visitor center. A portapotty is available in the parking lot.

Tower Rock Campground is nearby, and there are a lot of dispersed camping options on the forest roads, including some nice spots along the Cispus River.

What was once a short road walk may be a longer hike (described here) due to road conditions. At this original 1930s lookout with panoramic views of three of Washington's volcanoes, get a true sense of how vast the lookout network used to be—and how much has been lost.

ON THE TRAIL

The trail intersects in two places with Forest Road 28, so you could shave 0.7 or 1.1 miles off the hike if you find parking on the road. Alternately, it is sometimes possible to drive most of the way up to Burley Mountain via FR 77 then FR 7605, and park a half mile before the summit. But that road is commonly washed out and impassable by regular passenger vehicles. Check current conditions and amend your trip as necessary.

Start on the Covell Creek Trail #228. The trail is flat, shady, and pleasant, with ferns, fir, maple, and Oregon grape. In 0.1 mile, reach the edge of Covell Creek and follow the trail as it jogs left (east). At 0.25 mile when you reach a junction, stay left toward Cispus. But instead of walking all the way to the road, walk behind the buildings before getting back on the trail to your right at 0.5 mile and 1355 feet. You go up a little incline before getting some flat trail again.

Reach FR 28 in 0.7 mile. Walk straight across the road and pick up the trail. After a little more forest walking, you'll cross FR 28 one more time at 1.1 miles and 1565 feet. Cross the road and jump back on the trail, signed as #256 to Burley Mountain. There is room for about two or three cars to park at this point where the trail crosses the road. In 150 feet, you will reach a sign that tells you there is a waterfall in 1 mile and FR 7605 in 3 miles. The trail now starts to climb more steadily, and becomes thick with salal.

You reach the first switchback at 1.4 miles with the sound of the creek flowing below and pretty maples overhanging the trail. Enjoy a last flat, easy section—once you cross Covell Creek, it will be an upward haul for more than 5 miles. At 1.9 miles, you approach the sound of the creek and reach an overgrown creekside section, thick with salmonberries. Cross the small creek on a makeshift log bridge at 2 miles and 2047 feet, and again about 100 feet later at a beautiful waterfall. The trail now starts switchbacking uphill. At 2.15 miles, there is a spur to the right for the Angel Falls Loop Trail #228B. Stay straight.

Reach the road to Burley Mountain, FR 7605, at 4 miles and around 4000 feet. Take note of this trail intersection, and mark it with rocks or sticks if needed; it's surprisingly easy to miss on your way back. Turn left (south) to start walking up the tree-lined gravel road. At 6 miles, views to the right (west) start to open up toward Strawberry Mountain and the green expanse of the Cascade foothills.

At 6.4 miles, reach a signed T intersection at 5000 feet. Follow the sign, staying left for Burley Mountain, as the road now does a hard switchback. At 6.7 miles, the lookout will come into view. At 6.8 miles, catch your first view to the right (which is now east). There is a parking area at 7 miles, which is where you would park if the road were open, and you only had to walk the last half mile. Pass through an old gate at 7.1 miles. You're almost there!

Reach the top at 7.5 miles and 5304 feet. Take in this view from an amazing perch that's pretty much smack in the middle of three volcanoes, with foothills and the rest of the southern Cascades all around. The lookout itself is a fourteen-foot L-4 ground house from 1934, now listed on the National Historic Lookout Register. In

Burley Mountain Lookout

the summer, you are likely to find the lookout unlocked. Inside there are two bed platforms, a counter, sink, bench, woodbox, woodstove, and the firefinder stand.

You may find some historical reading material about Burley Mountain on photo-copied pages inside. It's chock-full of fascinating history, like the fact that Burley was once part of a sixty-lookout network in the Gifford Pinchot National Forest. The lookout staff would typically start working on trails and phone lines in May, with the goal of getting the structure inhabited by July 1 and keeping it staffed through Labor Day. Because of Burley's central location near the Randle Ranger District, it was key to the radio communication system. The staff at this lookout had a primary responsibility of relaying radio messages; fire detection was secondary. The reading material also notes that back in those days, the radios used a lot of battery power but did not reach very far. While other lookouts from that era were being removed in the 1960s, Burley was left intact as a communication site until the early 1970s. The introduction of radio repeaters eventually rendered that job obsolete, and the lookout was abandoned for about a decade, during which one wall collapsed and the building was vandalized.

On its fiftieth birthday in 1984, the lookout was repaired through a joint effort by local volunteers and the US Forest Service. After that, it was staffed either by volunteers or employees during the summer and was used as a rental in the off-season for a while. Local volunteers made another restoration push in the summer of 2009.

Thanks to the interpretive plaques at the summit, you get a keener sense here than perhaps at any other lookout of just how many lookout sites there used to be. Lining the horizon to the east you can see Cispus Point, Hawkeye Point (in Goat Rocks Wilderness), Tongue Mountain, Hamilton Buttes, Sunrise and McCoy peaks, and Mount Adams—and all of these summits are former lookout locations. It's almost mind-boggling. (Yes, there was actually a lookout at the 12,276-foot summit of Mount Adams, which lasted a whopping three years.) There are more to the north too, and two still have lookouts: Watch Mountain over Randle and High Rock. Tatoosh used to have one. You also see Kiona Peak, Purcell Mountain, Mount Rainier, Pompey Peak, Twin Sisters, and South Point. Looking southwest you can see Mount St. Helens, Strawberry Mountain, French Butte, and Badger Peak. Want to guess how many lookouts are left in the Gifford Pinchot now? Three.

Return the way you came.

39 JUMP OFF MOUNTAIN

YEAR CONSTRUCTED	LOOKOUT ACCESS	LOCATION
1958	Open to public for day use	Okanogan-Wenatchee National Forest, Naches Ranger District

Roundtrip distance: 7.4 miles
Elevation gain: 1550 feet
Lookout elevation: 5670 feet
Maps: Green Trails Rimrock No. 304; USGS Tieton Basin and Foundation Ridge
GPS coordinates: N 46° 37' 20" W 121° 04' 08"
Permits and fees: None

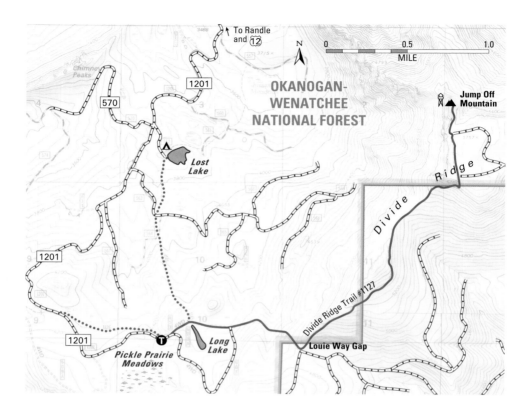

GETTING TO THE TRAILHEAD

From the intersection of State Route 131 and US Highway 12 in Randle, follow US 12 east for 52.7 miles, passing Rimrock Lake. Turn right (south) onto Tieton Reservoir Road and follow it for 1.9 miles. Turn left onto Forest Road 570; after 0.2 mile veer left at the fork to stay on FR 570. Follow it for another 2.6 miles. Reach an intersection, where straightish will take you to Lost Lake Campground. Stay right, turning onto FR 1201 and follow it for 2.8 miles until the wide, gravel road ends and the road narrows considerably. Parking is available on the side of the road. There is more camping just ahead.

In an area used by all-terrain-vehicle enthusiasts, this lookout has been nearly lost to hikers. But it's worth the trek to a cool vantage point where east meets west—Mount Rainier, Goat Rocks, and green foothills to one side and rocky cliffs and the dry expanse of the Yakima Valley to the other.

ON THE TRAIL

Even though the map says "4WD," I do not recommend trying to drive this section, even with four-wheel drive. It's too narrow, overgrown, steep, and deeply rutted for most vehicles. Since you are probably not starting out in an ATV, a jeep, or a sportster motorcycle, you will have to walk on the road for a ways before reaching the hiking trail. But don't worry; there is an extensive network of ATV roads back here, meaning it's unlikely that you'll run into many, if any, motorized vehicles on your walk. It does mean, though, that you may be walking up some steep hills through deep, powdery dirt.

At 1.2 miles, you reach Louie Way Gap, an open, flat, grassy area at around 4780 feet. Turn left (north) at the four-way intersection onto what looks like more of a faint jeep road than a trail. This is apparently Divide Ridge Trail #1127, though I did not see it labeled. The terrain stays open a little while longer, carpeted with sage and yarrow. By 2.25 miles, the road narrows into a trail, and you enter the woods, heading up Divide Ridge. You'll get your first view of the lookout through the trees.

At 2.4 miles, the trail starts descending slightly. At 2.5 miles there is a fantastic viewpoint to the left (west), overlooking Rimrock Lake, the Cascade foothills, cool cliffs and rocky outcroppings, and Mount Rainier. Once you've soaked in the beauty and are ready, continue on. You start climbing again at 2.8 miles and 5375 feet. Soon views will begin to open up to the right. You are on an open slope that feels more arid as you pick your way over talus and past asters.

Jump Off Mountain Lookout

Jump Off Mountain Lookout from the trail

At around 3 miles you start to crest the slope and see old barbed wire. You're now entering a dry field of low, scrubby bitterbrush and will pass through an old, fallen-down gate and fencing. At 3.2 miles and 5640 feet you meet the jeep road. Continue straightish on the road and enjoy this beautiful ridgetop plateau—open, grassy, and lovely. At 3.5 miles when you encounter a spur, stay to the left to stick to the road. Arrive at the lookout at 3.7 miles.

The lookout is open to the public, but, unfortunately, it has seen better days. There are holes in the walls, which are either covered up by plexiglass or plywood, and it does not have traditional shutters. Some of the glass windows remain, but others are shattered onto the floor, with the empty space boarded up. The linoleum is peeling upward in deep layers. On the plus side, the staircase has been recently replaced, and the wood is new, and the steps, sturdy.

The first lookout on this site was built around 1923: a D-6 cupola cab. Sometime in the 1930s, that was replaced by a classic design from that era: the L-4 cab. Then in 1958, the flat cab that you see today was built. It's currently maintained through volunteer efforts by a local motor club.

What the lookout lacks in structural beauty it makes up for in beautiful surroundings. This is a pretty amazing vantage point at almost 6000 feet, where east transitions to west. Mount Rainier looms, Rimrock Lake sparkles, and the Yakima Valley spreads out grand and golden.

Take the time to explore the large summit area. You may notice that the lookout is built on basalt, and right below it is a cliffside of pretty columnar basalt. Just southeast of the lookout is the old privy platform, with the fallen walls on the ground next to it.

Return the way you came.

40 RED MOUNTAIN

YEAR CONSTRUCTED	LOOKOUT ACCESS	LOCATION
1959	Closed to public; catwalk accessible	Gifford Pinchot National Forest, Mount Adams Ranger District

Roundtrip distance: 6.8 miles
Elevation gain: 1620 feet
Lookout elevation: 4965 feet
Map: Green Trails Indian Heaven No. 365S
GPS coordinates: N 45° 54' 30" W 121° 11' 18"
Permits and fees: None

GETTING TO THE TRAILHEAD

From the junction with Interstate 5 in Vancouver, Washington, travel east on State Route 14 for 48.8 miles, and turn north onto Wind River Highway. Drive this road for 11.5 miles, passing through the town of Carson. Turn right (east) onto Old State Road (passing the road the first time you see it at 10.1 miles), and follow it for 0.1 mile, then turn left (north) on Panther Creek Road. Soon Panther Creek Road becomes Forest Road 65. Follow it for 10.9 miles and turn right at the intersection

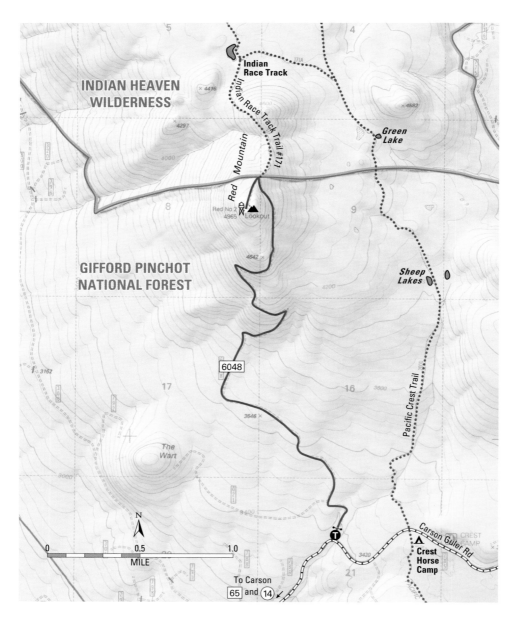

with Carson Guler Road (FR 60). Continue for 1.5 miles until you see a gate on the left. Park near the gate (but don't block it), and be careful parking by this road as it's on a turn. Camping is available along both FR 60 and FR 65, and also at Panther Creek Campground.

This pleasant hike follows an abandoned road up a volcanic mountain to the site of the first fire lookout in Western Washington.

ON THE TRAIL

Start by walking around the gate onto the gravel road of Forest Road 6048. At first the way is wide, the grade, gentle. Evergreen trees flank the sides of the road as you walk in and out of sun and shade. Small plants such as wild strawberry and ferns line the ground.

At 0.8 mile, you will reach a sign on the ground that says, "Primitive Road." Even though it's fallen over, don't doubt the sign's wisdom. There is a ton of blowdown for the next mile and a half or so. Be prepared to go over, under, or around fallen logs in an array of sizes on the road.

You'll ascend about 1100 feet in the first 2.6 miles. Then the views finally start to open up to the east and south. Gaze into Oregon at Mount Hood to the southeast, and if it's really clear, Mount Jefferson. At 3.15 miles Mount Adams appears large and looming to the northeast, just as you approach the intersection with the Indian Race Track Trail #171 on your right (north).

Red Mountain Lookout with Mount Hood

Red Top Mountain Lookout tower frames Mount Adams.

Here, the road turns sharply south, and the lookout and garage come into view at 3.3 miles. You pass the garage, and the trail switchbacks a few times up the slope of the last remaining bit of summit. Be careful to stay on the trail and not trample vegetation. You reach the lookout at 3.4 miles and 4965 feet. It's an R-6 wooden flattop fifteen-foot cab on a ten-foot timber tower. The lookout itself is locked, but you can ascend the 15 steps to take in the 360-degree views from the catwalk. It's an amazing vantage point to see five volcanoes—Mounts Adams, Rainier, St. Helens, Hood, and Jefferson. The sloping, green, Cascade fir–covered foothills are a striking contrast against the imposing, pointy, snowcapped peaks. Of volcanic origin, Red Mountain is named, unsurprisingly, for its volcanic-red pumice rocks.

This is the fourth lookout structure on this site, whose history started very early for Washington fire lookouts: there was an eight-foot-by-eight-foot wooden cabin here way back in 1910. Sometime after 1919 a cupola cab was constructed, and in 1935, during the CCC era, an L-4 cab was built, along with a garage.

In 1942 and 1943, Red Mountain was staffed twenty-four hours a day as an Aircraft Warning Service station during World War II, before the days of widespread radar use in the United States. At that time, the garage was used to store firewood, and a small sleeping room was added to one side as AWS staff living quarters, to

OPPOSITE *CCC-era garage, used for storage and AWS sleeping quarters, with Mount Rainier beyond*

accommodate the person during off-duty hours. According to Ray Kresek in *Fire Lookouts of the Northwest*, a husband-and-wife team worked as guards for one year, starting in October 1942. They made round-the-clock telephone calls and radio checks, though an enemy plane was never heard. In December that year they experienced temperatures as low as minus thirteen degrees Fahrenheit, and in January they got twenty feet of snowfall, which stayed at that depth for two months. Postings in a fire lookout in the summer can be demanding; but postings to a lookout year-round require tough-as-nails, determined folks who deserve our gratitude for their stalwart service.

In 1959, the lookout you see today was built, and is typical of the designs that replaced the L-4 lookouts. In 2006, a winter windstorm blew the roof completely off the lookout, and it was repaired by the US Forest Service. The lookout is no longer staffed. Today at the summit the garage is still standing, now used for storage. There is a shipping container with mounted solar panels, a radio tower making an incessant humming noise, and a large propane tank.

Return the way you came.

41 KLOSHE NANITCH AND NORTH POINT

YEARS CONSTRUCTED	LOOKOUT ACCESS		LOCATION
Late 1920s and 1939	Closed to public; viewing platform accessible at Kloshe Nanitch		Olympic National Forest, Pacific Ranger District

Roundtrip distance: 0.8 mile

Elevation gain: 190 feet

Lookout elevation: 3160 feet (Kloshe Nanitch); 3340 feet (North Point)

Map: USGS Snider Peak

GPS coordinates: N 48° 04' 52" W 124° 04' 46"

Permits and fees: None, contact Forks Office for more information

GETTING TO THE TRAILHEAD

From Port Angeles, take US Highway 101 west for 37.5 miles. Turn north (right) onto West Snider Road, signed for Olympic National Forest—Snider Work Center. Follow

North Point Lookout, now a communications center

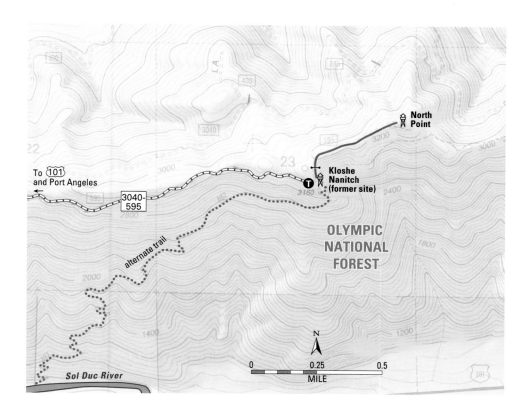

the paved road for 0.4 mile to the Snider Work Center, and turn left into the camp, signed for Forest Road 3041. From here drive behind the work center and follow the gravel FR 3041 for 5.2 miles, staying (straight) right when the road intersects with FR 3040. Follow FR 3040 for 0.4 mile until the road forks, and then stay right to FR 3040-595. Continue on this road for 1.3 miles until you reach the parking area for Kloshe Nanitch Lookout site. Park here (privy available) or continue a couple hundred feet to park by a gate at the "trailhead" for North Point.

There is camping available at Fairholme Campground at Lake Crescent (in the Olympic National Park) or at Klahowya Campground at the West Snider Road turnoff, just off US 101 (in the Olympic National Forest).

Two for one! On the northern edge of the Olympic Peninsula, start your short walk at a stunning viewpoint—former site of a lookout—before continuing up the road to where another lookout stands.

View toward the Olympics from Kloshe Nanitch and North Point

ON THE TRAIL

The trailhead for North Point is basically the parking area for Kloshe Nanitch, with parking for about four cars. A constructed ramp and viewing platform remain where the Kloshe Nanitch Lookout used to be, on a point along Snider Ridge. Kloshe Nanitch was one of the very earliest lookouts constructed in Washington State, originally built as a D-6 wooden-cupola cabin in the 1920s. It was accessible only by trail at first, then the CCC built a road in the 1930s. The structure was destroyed in the 1960s, and a replica was built in the same spot in 1996 and turned into an interpretive site and rental building. Unfortunately, the building was extensively vandalized and was removed in 2012.

This is a unique spot among lookouts: the structure is gone but the viewing platform is lovely, and from here you can look northeast along the ridge where North Point, your next destination, is visible. You can also see south into the Olympic Mountains, including Mount Olympus, and look down to Lake Crescent and the Sol Duc River.

From Kloshe Nanitch, keep walking up the road or drive just a couple hundred feet farther until you reach a locked gate. Park on the side of the road, without blocking the gate. The "hike" officially starts here. Walk up the gravel road hemmed with evergreen trees on both sides. It's a short and pleasant stroll that gently slopes upward.

You reach the summit at 0.4 mile and 3340 feet. The original L-4 structure was built in 1939, when the use of Kloshe Nanitch was in decline. The lookout site was moved this slight distance away—to the northeast—possibly because it had a better view north toward the Strait of Juan de Fuca or possibly because radio-signal reception was better here. Like many of the lookouts on the Pacific Coast, the North Point Lookout was used in the Aircraft Warning Service in World War II.

The building was officially abandoned by 1969. It saw some rough years after that, falling into neglect and disrepair and subjected to vandalism. It was repurposed as a communications center in 1992, and is now standing in a visually chaotic jumble of towers, wires, cables, generators, rooftop solar panels, a cell tower, and other shed-like structures. It's a bit of an eyesore—this is not a hike you do to soak in the beautiful summit area. But what the summit lacks in natural beauty is made up for in interesting history, accessibility, and lovely Olympic views. You have vistas sweeping from the southeast right to the southwest. Take in Bigler Mountain, Hunger Mountain, Rugged Ridge, and Sore Thumb.

Return the way you came.

42 PYRAMID MOUNTAIN

YEAR CONSTRUCTED	LOOKOUT ACCESS		LOCATION
1942	Open to public		Olympic National Park

Roundtrip distance: 7.4 miles
Elevation gain: 2400 feet
Lookout elevation: 3100 feet
Map: Custom Correct Map: Lake Crescent—Happy Lake Ridge
GPS coordinates: N 48° 3' 56" W 123° 8' 25"
Permits and fees: None; Wilderness Information Center

GETTING TO THE TRAILHEAD
From Port Angeles follow US Highway 101 west for 27 miles to Fairholme on the western end of Lake Crescent (Milepost 221). Turn right on Camp David Jr. Road (a.k.a. North Shore Road) and proceed for 3 miles to a trailhead with shoulder parking

before the North Shore Picnic Area. There is space for around twenty cars and two ADA spaces. The trail begins on the north side of the road. Camping is available on Lake Crescent at Fairholme Campground.

> This quintessential Olympic Peninsula hike of river valley, moss, and verdant trailsides that tower above Lake Crescent visits a lookout outlier with a view of the ocean—it was actually a post to watch for wartime planes, not for fires.

ON THE TRAIL

Start on the north side of the road, signed for Pyramid Mountain Trail, and follow the graded, paved walkway. You reach Spruce Railroad Trail in 0.1 mile and cross it, following the sign for Pyramid Mountain. Now you step into a verdant, lush Olympic forest, with a soft, humuslike trail surface and plants all around: big sword fern, flattish hemlocks, cedar, salal, Oregon grape, and carpets of moss.

Start going up slowly and steadily, getting into a green canopy of alder and maple. Looking south you can catch glimpses of the lake through the trees. You'll even see a few Pacific madrones, and it's as if ecology is sharing an invisible secret: even though you can't see the ocean, you know it must be close, because madrones like salt air and tend to grow only near salt water. You'll also see bracken fern, wild rose, vanilla leaf, and a few old-growth trees.

By 1.4 miles, the trail begins trending a little more to the north, hugging the eastern side of the slope. Cross a creek at 1.5 miles, and another at 1.75 miles, where there is a slide in a creek—watch your step. Consider it a warm-up for the really dicey

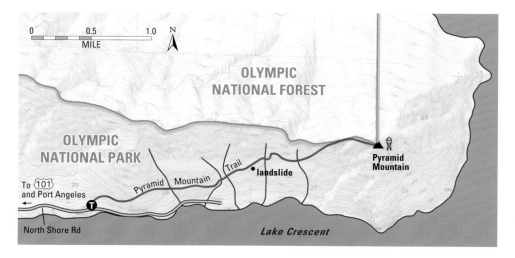

Pyramid Mountain Lookout

section that comes at 1.9 miles and around 1670 feet: a landslide (marked on map). A huge swath of the slope is gone, leaving a section of bare dirt and rocks. A narrow, improvised trail now traverses the slide, and it's not too bad if you just take it one step at a time. Some people (myself included) may find comfort in the added stability of a trekking pole or walking stick to cross this section. Do not attempt to cross if you have vertigo, and it's not advisable for children. Don't expect that the trail will ever be repaired, as it would likely slide again. On the plus side, the openness means it has a beautiful view to the right (south) down to Lake Crescent and to Aurora Ridge.

Once you get to the other side, it becomes clear that this trail is lower than the original route, and the new route has to now switchback up steeply to meet up with the original trail. Continue along the switchbacks at a steady climb until you reach the ridgeline at 2300 feet and 2.75 miles.

The trail flattens slightly as you follow the ridgeline east, and now you also get views to the north! Note that this area is incredibly thick with dense salal, so you might get drenched if the vegetation is at all damp.

At 2.9 miles you briefly cross the boundary from the national park into the national forest. By 3 miles the understory is less dense, and the trail starts switchbacking up the backside of the ridge. Starting at 3.3 miles, keep your eye out for side trails; if you have

Hiker on Pyramid Mountain Trail

the time and the inclination, there are several nice little viewpoint turnoff spots. If you don't want to lose momentum by detouring, don't worry; you'll reach a spot at 3.6 miles where the ridge view opens up, and you can look south again from a rocky outcropping.

You head back into the trees for a last little push, and reach the lookout at 3.7 miles and 3100 feet. It's a simple wooden structure built in 1942 and abandoned by 1945. It's a short amount of time, but, not coincidentally, spans the years that the United States was watching for enemy warplanes during World War II. It was one of thirteen enemy-airplane spotter cabins used on the Olympic Peninsula during the war.

This cabin is unique among the lookouts in this book. Instead of windows on all sides, it has solid sides and two windows that are now partially covered in plastic. The walls are marked with graffiti, but the inside is clean. It's a sturdy, unexpected relic of a bygone era, perched on a stunning vantage point. The summit area has enough space to sit down, have a snack, and take in the view of Aurora Peak to the south and Storm King to the southeast.

Return the way you came.

43 DODGER POINT

YEAR CONSTRUCTED	LOOKOUT ACCESS	LOCATION
1933	Closed to public; staffed as needed by National Park Service	Olympic National Park

Roundtrip distance: 28 miles
Elevation gain: 4890 feet
Lookout elevation: 5760 feet
Map: Green Trails Mt. Olympus No. 134
GPS coordinates: N 47° 58' 4" W 123° 25' 2"
Permits and fees: Day-use fee (good for seven days) payable at booth on Olympic Hot Springs Road or annual park or interagency pass; backcountry permit required for overnight stays (available at Wilderness Information Center in Port Angeles)

GETTING TO THE TRAILHEAD

From Port Angeles, drive US Highway 101 west 9 miles to Olympic Hot Springs Road. Turn left and continue 4.1 miles to Whiskey Bend Road; veer left onto it and continue for another 4.1 miles to the Whiskey Bend Trailhead. Privy available.

Dodger Point Lookout

This overnight takes you to the most remote lookout still standing in the Olympics, with jaunts along the mighty Elwha River, forested switchbacks, expansive views, and primo spots for subalpine camping.

ON THE TRAIL

Welcome to Whiskey Bend Trailhead, a portal into the depths of the Olympics. Nearly a dozen trails start from here, ranging from short out-and-backs to a 44-mile traverse across the mountain range. As such, be prepared for a lot of trail junctions, but everything is well signed.

Start on a fairly flat section in a forest of salal, Oregon grape, hemlock, fir, vanilla leaf, and slide alder. You are high above the Elwha River, and though you can't see it, you can hear it and sense the big valley below. Continue in the dense forest before views open up a bit to your right (southwest) at a signed overlook at 0.9 mile. You catch a glimpse of the river before the trail starts dropping a bit at 1.1 miles. You will eventually cross the Elwha, so be prepared to lose some elevation before the real climbing starts. In a couple hundred more feet, you reach the junction for Rica Canyon to the right; stay left. At 1.6 miles is a junction for Krause Bottom to the right; again, stay left.

You will reach another junction at 2 miles; this time stay right toward Humes Meadow and Dodger Point. To the left are Lillian Camp and Elkhorn Camp. Michael's Cabin is in a meadow immediately to the right of the junction. Built in 1937, it's a fun

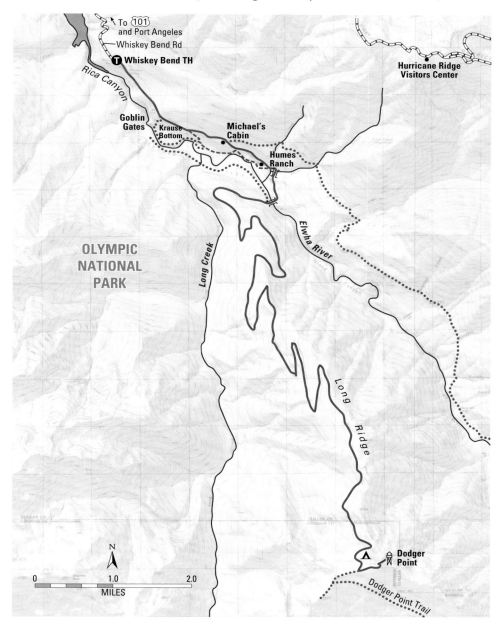

Olympic peaks from Dodger Point Trail

place to explore or take quick shelter from rain. It's sturdy and in good shape, empty of furniture, and a bit grimy inside. The cabin is named after a man who made his living by hunting cougars and other predators in the area and by maintaining trails and phone lines. Note that campfires and camping are prohibited within 100 feet of the structure.

As you go on from here, the vegetation starts to feel even more damp and river valleyish: moss, ferns, and verdant maples abound. The next junction is at 2.3 miles. Left is to Dodger Point and right is to Humes Ranch. For the more direct route, stay left, but going right is an option, as it meets back up with the main trail and is nearly the same mileage. I recommend taking the main trail in, and then taking this alternate route on the way back if you feel like changing things up.

Just after the junction is a bridge that has, uh, seen better days. A huge western red cedar fell and smashed it in half. Crossing isn't too hard, but you do have to climb up over the log. At 2.5 miles, look for a cabin through the trees to your right. At 2.7 miles, the main trail meets back up with the Humes Ranch Trail; take note of this junction if you want to follow the alternate route on your way back. Right would take you to the ranch; stay left, signed for Dodger Point.

Cross a bridge over a creek here, and at 2.9 miles you will catch a nice view of the Elwha River. The trail continues at a fairly steep drop until you reach the bridge over the river at 3.3 miles and 875 feet. You are now about 300 feet lower than where you started. Take in the view of the river valley from the metal-and-wood suspension bridge and marvel at the free-flowing river below you. The Elwha was dammed without a fish ladder in 1911, cutting off one of the most significant salmon runs in Washington State. By the 1980s, a significant percentage of the local population felt that the electricity generated was not substantial, but the environmental impact was. Congress enacted legislation in 1992 authorizing the dam's removal. It took almost two decades of public forums, reviews, and planning before the six-month demolition process began on the Elwha Dam in 2011, and by 2014 the Glines Canyon Dam had also been removed. The Elwha is being monitored by scientists as it transitions back to being a free-flowing river.

Those first few miles were your warm-up. Have a snack and stretch your legs, because now it's time to climb. Cross the river, and the trail starts switchbacking up the other side. For the next almost 10 miles, you make your way steadily up Long Ridge, gaining approximately 500 feet per mile. This section is shady and thick with sword fern, and in places very dense with salal overgrowing the trail. You'll pass a flattish area with a possible campsite at 4.6 miles. At 5.7 miles, you can start to see Hurricane Ridge through the trees to the northeast.

Hikers on Dodger Point Trail

At 8.3 miles, the trail makes a hairpin turn to the left. At 8.75 miles you'll reach 3500 feet, and a sign reminds you that open fires are prohibited above that elevation—stoves only.

You've been working hard going uphill for the last 7 miles, and views finally start to open up a little at 10.2 miles, with peaks to the south. Within the next mile or two, you will pass a few mossy, spongy spots where natural springs cross the trail. It might be little more than a damp section, but there are one or two places where the water pools enough to collect and treat for drinking. Then there is an actual creek around 11 miles where water flows more steadily.

At 11.5 miles, you get some more views to the right, and start to see white knobby logs and trunks, as well as blueberries. At this point, you will begin to feel like you are getting somewhere, with a more subalpine feel—meadows, lupine, mountain heather, and little trees. Just after 12 miles is a campsite on your right.

You'll soon catch a view of Mount Olympus to the southwest as the trail turns rockier and passes through screelike sections. Noble firs appear, and some low rock walls line the trail. You've been in the trees a lot throughout, but this section is really neat. Reach the heart of the hike at around 12.7 miles—a stunning, unique bowl-meadow area with many mountains behind. While the tarns are a possible water source, all that standing water makes it major mosquito zone in the summer. Do your best to walk on established trails in this fragile area.

After the trail traverses above the tarns, you start climbing again. Even though this area is mostly sloped, there are some flat spots with established campsites at around 13 miles. You are allowed to camp anywhere as long as it's a durable surface (rock or dirt, not vegetation). If you look up, you can see the ridgeline above that the lookout is on, but it's set back from the edge and not visible yet.

Continue on to the junction at 13.5 miles. Stay left to go east and uphill. This is the last push! It's a hard but nice one: sloping meadows and sweeping views with sweet victory feeling inspiringly close. Finally, after this serious haul, reach the lookout at 14 miles and 5760 feet.

The structure is a fourteen-foot L-4 ground house from 1933. Like many of the lookouts on the Olympic Peninsula, Dodger Point was used as an Aircraft Warning Service station during World War II. It was added to the National Register of Historic Places in 2007. It's closed to the public, but you can enjoy the views from the grassy summit. It's still used by the Park Service on an as-needed basis. Back in the day, the staff used a crank phone to call down to the nearest guard station, probably Elwha, Elkhorn, or Hayes River. Rangers watched for fires, but also acted as a backcountry presence to deter tree poaching. Relish the serene solitude of being so deep in the Olympics, and then return the way you came.

44 NED HILL

YEAR CONSTRUCTED	LOOKOUT ACCESS		LOCATION
Approximately 1933	Closed to public; rickety platform is unsafe to climb		Olympic National Forest, Hood Canal Ranger District

Roundtrip distance: 2 miles
Elevation gain: 910 feet
Lookout elevation: 3458 feet
Map: Green Trails Tyler Peak No. 136
GPS coordinates: N 47° 58' 4" E 123° 48' 43"
Permits and fees: None

GETTING TO THE TRAILHEAD

From Sequim take US Highway 101 to the Taylor Cutoff Road, and take a left. The road veers right and changes to the Lost Mountain Road at 2.5 miles, continuing for 5 miles. Keep an eye out for Forest Road 2870 (a.k.a. Slab Camp Road—a bit hidden),

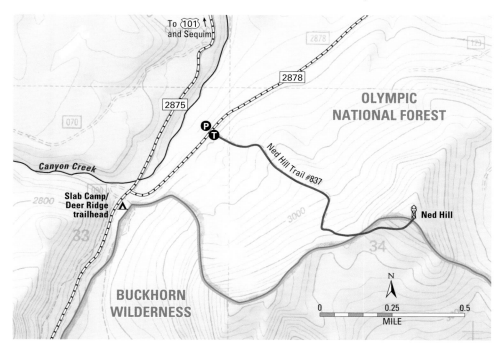

going left where a "Dead End" sign is located. Follow FR 2870 for 0.8 mile to FR 2875 on the right. Take FR 2875 for 3.4 miles to a wide intersection at the Slab Camp/Deer Ridge Trailhead (camping available here). Go left, now on FR 2878. Follow it for 0.3 mile to the Ned Hill Trailhead on the right. The sign is set back in the woods a bit and parking is a bit farther up the road.

This very short hike, packed with native rhododendrons, visits the most primitive lookout still standing—an enticing, improbable, rickety tower and sagging platform.

ON THE TRAIL

Start at Ned Hill Trail #837. As you would expect on the Olympic Peninsula, this trail is incredibly green, almost glowing. You are immediately in a forest of towering hemlocks, gigantic pink-blossomed Pacific rhododendron, lush salal, wild rose, ferns, and Oregon grape. Some of the rhododendrons are draped with moss, which may make you do a double take. Is this a forest or a garden? In a unique blending of the two, enjoy Washington's state flower that blooms in May and June. This makes an excellent early season hike when the higher lookouts are still buried in snow.

The trail starts by climbing steadily for the first half mile. It's a solid climb, but you'll pass three wooden benches along the way to stop and rest your weary legs if you need, and they are spaced about every quarter mile or so. This trail does not use switchbacks, and considering there is a flat part, the parts that go uphill are no joke. Even though it's short, you may want trekking poles, especially for a couple spots on the way down.

After 0.5 mile, enjoy a short flat bit. Then around 0.8 mile, climb steeply again. The understory starts to open up, and moss dangles from the hemlocks. The trees also thin out a bit, and you get views of neighboring mountains to the south and southeast in the Buckhorn Wilderness, such as Peak B and Tyler and Maynard peaks. In season, you'll see some new flowers in this open bit, such as Indian paintbrush and western trillium, and you'll pass the fourth bench of the trail, which once afforded grand views looking south, but the trees have surely grown since then, obscuring much of the vista.

You reach the lookout in 1 mile after ascending 910 feet. To be honest, "lookout" is a generous term for the structure—and perhaps that makes it all the more endearing. This looks like a precarious fort that an enthusiastic teenager might have built on summer vacation. The tower is enclosed by a wooden fence; it's best to stay back and admire the history from afar.

OPPOSITE *Remnants of the Ned Hill Lookout platform*

Bench on the Ned Hill Trail

We don't know exactly when the platform was built, but there is a panoramic photo taken from it in 1935. Sometime earlier in the twentieth century, a big fire swept through the area around Maynard Peak and Ned Hill. Wising up, the US Forest Service stationed a guard on the Slab Camp Creek to the southeast of Ned Hill. The guard would use the platform on Ned Hill to scan the slopes of Maynard Peak and Mount Baldy and the Gray Wolf River valley. To the west 4 miles are Blue Mountain and Deer Park. To the north he could see the Strait of Juan de Fuca. The platform was eventually abandoned, tall trees grew up around it, and the Slab Camp Trail was no longer used. In 1994, the trail was reestablished thanks to volunteer efforts.

Return the way you came.

BONUS LOOKOUTS

MOUNT ADAMS

YEAR CONSTRUCTED: 1918
LOOKOUT ACCESS: Closed to public; in ruins and under snow most of the year
LOCATION: Gifford Pinchot National Forest, Mount Adams Ranger District

Lookout elevation: 12,276 feet
Permits and fees: Climbing permit
Getting there: Mountaineering

Yes, you read that right. The same Mount Adams that is our 12,280-foot snow-clad volcano. Seem like an extreme, unlikely, and possibly ineffective place for a fire lookout? If you answered yes to any of those questions, you'd be correct! In the early days of lookout-building fervor, they must have thought that if high is good, higher is better. Of course, they may not have taken into account that you're so far above the tree line that forests are pretty far away; you may actually be in or above clouds much of the day; and elevation means the structure will be covered by snow most of the year and pummeled by wind. But building it was an impressive feat. Remember, 12,276

feet is higher than airplanes flew at the time. To have a vantage point that far up truly was an accomplishment—one that the lookout staffers got to savor for a full three years before it was abandoned.

STELIKO POINT

YEAR CONSTRUCTED: 1947
LOOKOUT ACCESS: Closed to public; catwalk accessible
LOCATION: Wenatchee National Forest, Entiat Ranger District

Lookout elevation: 2586 feet
Permits and fees: None
Getting there: Drive up

FIRST BUTTE

YEAR CONSTRUCTED: 1938
LOOKOUT ACCESS: Closed to public
LOCATION: Okanogan National Forest, Methow Valley Ranger District

Lookout elevation: 5491 feet
Permits and fees: None
Getting there: Drive up

LOOKOUTS CHECKLIST

Use this list to track which lookouts you've visited and stay motivated to see them all.

NORTH

- ☐ Buck Mountain
- ☐ Copper Ridge
- ☐ Desolation Peak
- ☐ Funk Mountain
- ☐ Goat Peak
- ☐ Green Mountain
- ☐ Hidden Lake
- ☐ Lookout Mountain (Cascade River Road)
- ☐ Lookout Mountain (Methow Valley)
- ☐ Miners Ridge
- ☐ Mount Bonaparte
- ☐ Mount Constitution
- ☐ Mount Leecher
- ☐ Mount Pilchuck
- ☐ Monument 83
- ☐ North Mountain
- ☐ North Twentymile
- ☐ Park Butte
- ☐ Slate Peak
- ☐ Sourdough Mountain
- ☐ Three Fingers
- ☐ Winchester Mountain

CENTRAL

- ☐ Alpine Lookout
- ☐ Evergreen Mountain
- ☐ Granite Mountain
- ☐ Heybrook Mountain
- ☐ Red Top Mountain
- ☐ Sugarloaf Peak
- ☐ Thorp Mountain
- ☐ Tyee Mountain

SOUTH

- ☐ Burley Mountain
- ☐ Gobblers Knob
- ☐ High Rock
- ☐ Jump Off Mountain
- ☐ Kelly Butte
- ☐ Mount Fremont
- ☐ Red Mountain
- ☐ Shriner Peak
- ☐ Sun Top
- ☐ Tolmie Peak

OLYMPICS

- ☐ Dodger Point
- ☐ Kloshe Nanitch and North Point
- ☐ Ned Hill
- ☐ Pyramid Mountain

OPPOSITE *Park Butte Lookout at sunset*

APPENDIX: OTHER LOOKOUTS IN WASHINGTON

LOOKOUTS STILL STANDING

The hikes in this book include publicly accessible lookouts in the western half of Washington State. The lookouts listed below weren't covered because they are farther east, are not publicly accessible, or require technical skills (such as the summit of Mount Adams). Always research trail and road conditions thoroughly before attempting to visit these lookouts.

LOOKOUT	YEAR CONSTRUCTED	LOCATION
1. Aeneas Mountain	1980	Okanogan County
2. Armstrong Mountain	1939	Colville Reservation
3. Big Butte	1950	Umatilla National Forest
4. Clearwater Cabin (rental)	1938	Umatilla National Forest
5. Cody Butte	1931	Colville Reservation
6. Columbia Mountain	1914	Colville National Forest
7. Cornell Butte	1958	Okanogan National Forest
8. First Butte	1938	Okanogan National Forest
9. Franson Peak	1986	Ferry County
10. Gold Mountain	1986	Colville Reservation
11. Goodman Hill	1930s	Fort Lewis/Pierce County
12. Grizzly Mountain	1930	Colville Reservation
13. Indian Mountain	1953	Kaniksu National Forest
14. Johnny George	1938	Colville Reservation
15. Keller Butte	1964	Colville Reservation
16. Kitsap Lookout	1940s	Kitsap County
17. Knowlton Knob	1966	Okanogan County
18. Lookout Point	1976	Spokane County

OPPOSITE *Summit view from catwalk of Lookout Mountain Lookout (Cascade River Road)*

LOOKOUT	YEAR CONSTRUCTED	LOCATION
19. Lorena Butte	1974	Klickitat County
20. Lynx Mountain Cabin	1926	Colville Reservation
21. Meadow Butte	1944	Klickitat County
22. Mebee Pass	1934	Okanogan National Forest
23. Moses Mountain	1938	Colville Reservation
24. Mount Adams	1918	Gifford Pinchot National Forest/ Mount Adams Wilderness
25. Mount Spokane	1934	Mount Spokane State Park
26. Omak Mountain	1986	Colville Reservation
27. Oregon Butte	1931	Umatilla National Forest
28. Puyallup Ridge	1964	Pierce County
29. Quartz Mountain (rental)	1934	Mount Spokane State Park
30. Salmo Mountain	1964	Colville National Forest
31. Satus Peak	1976	Yakama Nation Reservation
32. Signal Peak	1964	Yakama Nation Reservation
33. South Baldy	1960	Kaniksu National Forest
34. Steliko Point	1947	Wenatchee National Forest
35. Strawberry Mountain	1938	Colville Reservation
36. Sullivan Mountain	1960	Colville National Forest
37. Table Rock	1949	Umatilla National Forest
38. Timber Mountain	1959	Colville National Forest
39. Tower Mountain	1975	Spokane Reservation
40. Tunk Mountain	1966	Okanogan County
41. Watch Mountain	1963	Gifford Pinchot National Forest
42. Wellpinit Mountain	1964	Spokane Reservation
43. Whitestone Ridge	1985	Colville Reservation
44. Whitmore L-4 Cab	1938	Colville Reservation
45. Whitmore Summit Tower	1964	Colville Reservation

RELOCATED LOOKOUTS OF WASHINGTON STATE

In addition to the lookouts still standing in their original locations, a handful of gems in the state have been relocated to museums, parks, and private property. The

Columbia Breaks Fire Interpretive Center property is very worthy of a visit. It hosts three relocated lookouts: Badger Mountain, Chelan Butte, and a replica of the one on Flattop Mountain, all of which are listed below. They have all been moved from their original homes and are now full of cool history and information. Don't worry about visiting hours; it's a self-guided tour around the property. From Entiat, drive north for 1 mile on US Highway 97 to 15037 and the interpretive center will be on your left.

LOOKOUT	YEAR CONSTRUCTED	LOCATION
1. Badger Mountain Lookout	1941	Columbia Breaks Fire Interpretive Center
2. Blyn Lookout	1960	Private property
3. Buttermilk Butte Lookout	1934	Private property
4. Chelan Butte Lookout	1939	Columbia Breaks Fire Interpretive Center
5. Chewelah Peak Lookout	1963	Private property
6. First Thought Lookout	1947	Orient Community Park
7. Flagstaff Mountain Lookout	1971	Stevens County
8. Flattop Mountain (replica)	1946	Columbia Breaks Fire Interpretive Center
9. Fosback Lookout	1965	Private property
10. Franson Peak Lookout	1950	Molson Museum
11. Goat Peak Lookout	1956	Private property
12. Graves Mountain Lookout	1955	Keller Heritage Center
13. Ray Kresek Lookout	1930s	Private property
14. Salmon River Ridge Lookout	1967	Buckley Foothills Historical Museum
15. Sekiu Mountain Lookout	1964	Forks Timber Museum
16. Stampede Pass Lookout	1934	Highline Public School District property
17. Stranger Mountain Lookout	1983	Colville Fairgrounds

RESOURCES

MANAGING AGENCIES

E.C. MANNING PROVINCIAL PARK, BC
www.env.gov.bc.ca/bcparks

GIFFORD PINCHOT NATIONAL FOREST
www.fs.usda.gov/main/giffordpinchot
Cowlitz Valley Ranger District,
   (360) 497-1100
Mount Adams Ranger District,
   (509) 395-3400

MORAN STATE PARK
http://parks.state.wa.us/547/Moran
(360) 376-2326
3572 Olga Road
Olga, WA 98279

MOUNT BAKER–SNOQUALMIE NATIONAL FOREST
www.fs.usda.gov/main/mbs
Darrington Ranger District,
   (360) 436-1155
Glacier Public Service Center,
   (360) 599-2714
Mount Baker Ranger District,
   (360) 856-5700
Skykomish Ranger District,
   (360) 677-2414

Snoqualmie Ranger District, Enumclaw,
   (360) 825-6585
Snoqualmie Ranger District, North
   Bend, (425) 888-1421
Verlot Public Service Center,
   (360) 691-7791

MOUNT RAINIER NATIONAL PARK
www.nps.gov/mora/index.htm
*Note: Any of these stations in Mount
Rainier National Park can assist visitors with permits and basic information
regarding any of the hikes located in this
park. For more specific information or
assistance, contact the designated station
listed for the hike.*
Carbon River Ranger Station,
   (360) 829-9639
Longmire Wilderness Information
   Center, (360) 569-6650
White River Wilderness Information
   Center, (360) 569-6670

NORTH CASCADES NATIONAL PARK
www.nps.gov/noca/index.htm
Park and Forest Information Center,
   Sedro-Woolley, (360) 854-7200

OPPOSITE *Morning shadow of Lookout Mountain Lookout (Methow Valley)*

Wilderness Information Center,
   Marblemount, (360) 854-7245
Ross Lake National Recreation Area
   is managed by the North Cascades
   National Park Service Complex.
Ross Lake Resort, (206) 386-4437

OKANOGAN-WENATCHEE NATIONAL FOREST

www.fs.usda.gov/main/okawen
Cle Elum Ranger District,
   (509) 852-1100
Entiat Ranger District, (509) 784-4700
Methow Valley Ranger District,
   (509) 996-4003
Naches Ranger District, (509) 653-1401
Tonasket Ranger District,
   (509) 486-2186
Wenatchee River Ranger District,
   (509) 548-2550

OLYMPIC NATIONAL FOREST

www.fs.usda.gov/main/olympic
Hood Canal Ranger District,
   (360) 765-2200
Pacific Ranger District, Forks Office,
   (360) 374-6522

OLYMPIC NATIONAL PARK

www.nps.gov/olym/planyourvisit/wic
   .htm
Wilderness Information Center, Port
   Angeles, (360) 565-3100

SUGGESTED READING

Hansen, Heather. *Wildfire: On the Front
   Lines with Station 8*. Seattle, WA:
   Mountaineers Books, 2018.

Kerouac, Jack. *The Dharma Bums*. New
   York: Penguin Books, 1958. Reprint
   2006.
Kresek, Ray. *Fire Lookouts of the
   Northwest*. Rev. ed. Fairfield, WA: Ye
   Galleon Press, 1985.
Spring, Ira, and Byron Fish. *Lookouts:
   Firewatchers of the Cascades and
   Olympics*. 2nd ed. Seattle, WA:
   Mountaineers Books, 1996.
Suiter, John. *Poets on the Peaks: Gary
   Snyder, Philip Whalen, and Jack
   Kerouac in the North Cascades*. New
   York: Counterpoint, 2002.

MAP RESOURCES

CALTOPO
http://caltopo.com

CASCADE ORIENTEERING CLUB
http://cascadeoc.org

GREEN TRAILS
https://greentrailsmaps.com

INTERNATIONAL TRAVEL MAPS AND BOOKS
www.itmb.ca

MAPTOWN
www.maptown.com

USGS
www.usgs.gov/products/maps
   /topo-maps
https://store.usgs.gov

ACKNOWLEDGMENTS

It takes a village to raise a book, and I'm incredibly thankful for all the people who have been a part of that community over the past few years. At the heart of the project was the hiking research, and many friends and family joined me on the trail. I'm so grateful for the conversation, enthusiasm, snacks, and knowledge they shared—and their patience with my constant note taking: Alice Bremner, Gabrielle Roesch-McNally, Tessa Hulls, Max Benson, Gretchen Deutschlander, Jacqueline Cramer, Alex Yates, Hannah Baughman, Brandon Adams, Tegan Callahan, Greg Kennedy, Jennifer Green, Laura Casali Smith with Emma and Aubrey Smith, Jesse Pickard with Freya and Finn Pickard, Kalianna Shearouse, Joe Green, Becca Hall, Matt Freedman, Ben Heneghan, Grant Cross, George Winn, Alyssa Seal, Kent Yoder, Carl Slimp, Riley Bosket, and Alex Castillo.

A big thank you to the people who contributed to this project in so many other ways, including providing hospitality, cozy places to write, delicious food, logistics help, high-clearance vehicles, photography expertise, lookout history, legal counsel, and/or moral support: Katie Cassidy and Alan Mooers, Brook Steussy-Edfelt and family, Greg Williamson, Anne Kagi and family, Tonya and Jesse Pickard, Laura and Chuck Smith, Jennifer and Larry Green, Adam Andrews, Matt Freedman, Alex Arroyo, Chris Thompson, Robert Kendall, Gary Knell, "Lightning" Bill Austin, Doug Wilcox and Michelle Mondot, Steph Abegg, Riley Bosket and family, Cassidy Grattan and Liz Donadio, and Jason Neuerburg.

Thank you to the Sierra Institute and the Washington Alpine Club for helping equip me with the confidence and skills to safely spend time in the mountains.

Sincerest gratitude to my copyeditor, Ginger Everhart, who wrangled my words and truly elevated this book with her thoughtful work. Huge thanks to Mountaineers Books editors Kate Rogers and Laura Shauger, who brought this project to life.

Thanks to Yesler for supporting me in the UW editing certificate, where I met the guest speaker who sparked the idea to write this guide.

My final shout-out goes to Will Taylor and Lindsey Newman for their unwavering love and support, and for making me feel at my most writerly.

INDEX

OPPOSITE *Native rhododendron on the Ned Hill Trail*